ONE-DISH
MEALS

Publications International, Ltd.

Photo credits: **Robert Holmes:** 4; **Mae Scanlan:** 40; **Lee Snider/Photo Images:** 164; **Tom Stack & Associates:** Joanne Lotter: 124; John Shaw: 6, 74, 100.

Front cover illustration by Barbara Kiwak.

Pictured on the front cover: Homestyle Chicken Pot Pie *(page 54)*.
Pictured on the back cover *(clockwise from top left):* Summer Sausage 'n' Egg Wedge *(page 174),* Vegetable Soup with Delicious Dumplings *(page 120)* and Smoked Sausage and Noodle Skillet *(page 154).*

ISBN: 0-7853-2941-2

Library of Congress Catalog Card Number: 98-66643

Manufactured in U.S.A.

8 7 6 5 4 3 2 1

ONE-DISH MEALS

KITCHEN CLIPS

The convenience of one-dish meals is unbeatable. Casseroles, skillet dishes, soups and stews are so helpful to a busy cook and make cleanup a breeze. And, they can be prepared ahead of time and frozen. Even though stir-fries can't be cooked ahead of time, the quick cooking times will have hungry eaters satisfied in no time. What a relief it is to know that on that really busy day you'll have a delicious home-cooked meal ready for your family in a flash.

Inside there are so many one-dish meals to choose from—creamy, comforting casseroles, super-fast stir-fries, simple, savory skillet dishes, and fabulous soups, stews and chilies in every chapter. You'll find all the traditional favorites marked with the "Country Classic" symbol throughout the chapters. Also spotlighted are "Lightened Up" recipes that make it easier to add more health conscious recipes to your everyday diet. Read on for helpful tips that will give you successful results with all of your one-dish meals.

Casseroles

Casserole cookware comes in a variety of shapes, sizes and materials. If the size isn't marked on the dish, it can be measured to determine the size. Round and oval casseroles are measured by volume, not inches, and are always listed by their quart capacity. Fill a measuring cup with water and pour it into an empty casserole. Repeat until the casserole is filled with water, keeping track of the amount of water added. The amount of water is equivalent to the size of the dish. Square and rectangular baking dishes are measured in inches. Use a ruler to measure across the top from the inside of one edge to the inside of the edge directly across.

If a recipe calls for a casserole size or shape that you don't have, check the following chart for a possible substitution. Substituting for similar sizes isn't a problem.

Substitution Guide

Casserole Capacity	Baking Dish Size	Cups
1 quart	8-inch pie plate	4
1½ quarts	8×8×1½-inch 11×7-inch	6
2 quarts	8×8×2-inch 9×9×1½-inch 9-inch deep-dish pie plate	8
2½ quarts	9×9×2-inch	10
3½ to 4 quarts	13×9-inch	14 to 16

Freezing Tips

Most casseroles are great candidates for freezing. Here's a helpful way to freeze a casserole without tying up all of your dishes. Line the casserole with plastic wrap, folding plastic wrap over the edges, and spray with nonstick cooking spray. Add the combined casserole ingredients; cover with plastic wrap and place in the freezer. When frozen, lift the food from the casserole by lifting the plastic wrap by the edges. Wrap airtight in freezer paper or place in a resealable plastic freezer food storage bag, removing as much air as possible to avoid freezer burn. Return the food to the freezer.

When you're ready to cook the food, remove it from the freezer and discard all plastic wrap. Place it in the original container, cover and place in the refrigerator to defrost. Bake the casserole in a preheated oven according to the recipe directions. You might have to bake 10 to 15 minutes more since the food is chilled.

Skillet Dishes

- Use a skillet with high sides that's large enough to contain all the ingredients.

- Keep cooked pasta and rice in the freezer for quick additions to skillet dishes.

- A well-stocked pantry and freezer will never leave you wondering what to make. They also eliminate last-minute dashes to the grocery store to pick up extra items.

Stir-Fries

- Carefully read the entire recipe and prepare all ingredients before beginning to cook.

- Cut ingredients into similar-size pieces so they cook at the same rate.

- A consistent, easily controlled heat source is important when stir-frying.

- Stir-fry with oils that can withstand high temperatures without burning, such as peanut, corn and soybean oils.

Soups & Stews

- Cut vegetables and meats into bite-size pieces.

- Cook pasta and rice separately and add it to the soup when ready to serve. This prevents the pasta or rice from overcooking and making the soup cloudy.

- Make an extra big batch and freeze it in separate containers for quick meals.

MEATY MEALS

Ham and Potato au Gratin

---

3 tablespoons butter or margarine
3 tablespoons all-purpose flour
2 cups milk
1½ cups (6 ounces) shredded Cheddar cheese
1 tablespoon Dijon mustard
2 cups HILLSHIRE FARM® Ham, cut into thin strips
1 package (24 ounces) frozen shredded hash brown potatoes, thawed
1 package (10 ounces) frozen chopped spinach, thawed and drained

Preheat oven to 350°F.

Melt butter in large saucepan over medium heat; stir in flour. Add milk. Cook and stir until bubbly; cook 1 minute more. Remove from heat. Stir in cheese and mustard; set aside.

Place ½ of Ham into ungreased medium casserole. Top ham with ½ of potatoes and ½ of milk mixture. Spoon spinach over top. Repeat layers with remaining ham, potatoes and milk mixture.

Bake, uncovered, 30 minutes or until heated through.   *Makes 8 servings*

Ham and Potato au Gratin

Beef Mole Tamale Pie

1½ pounds ground chuck
1 medium onion, chopped
1 green bell pepper, chopped
2 cloves garlic, minced
1¼ cups medium-hot salsa
1 package (10 ounces) frozen whole kernel corn, partially thawed
1 tablespoon unsweetened cocoa powder
2 teaspoons ground cumin
1 teaspoon dried oregano leaves
1½ teaspoons salt, divided
¼ teaspoon ground cinnamon
2 cups (8 ounces) shredded Monterey Jack or Cheddar cheese
⅓ cup chopped fresh cilantro
1 cup all-purpose flour
¾ cup yellow cornmeal
3 tablespoons sugar
2 teaspoons baking powder
⅔ cup milk
3 tablespoons butter, melted
1 egg, beaten
Cilantro leaves, chili pepper and sour cream for garnish

Preheat oven to 400°F. Spray 11×7-inch baking dish with nonstick cooking spray. Brown ground chuck with onion, bell pepper and garlic in large deep skillet or Dutch oven over medium heat until meat just loses its pink color. Pour off drippings. Stir in salsa, corn, cocoa, cumin, oregano, 1 teaspoon salt and cinnamon. Bring to a boil. Reduce heat to medium-low; simmer, uncovered, 8 minutes, stirring occasionally. Remove from heat; stir in cheese and cilantro. Spread in prepared dish.

Combine flour, cornmeal, sugar, baking powder and remaining ½ teaspoon salt in large bowl. Add milk, butter and egg; stir just until dry ingredients are moistened. Drop by spoonfuls evenly over meat mixture; spread batter evenly with spatula.

Bake 15 minutes. *Reduce oven temperature to 350°F.* Bake 20 minutes or until topping is light brown and filling is bubbly. Let stand 5 minutes before serving. Garnish, if desired.

Makes 6 servings

Baked Cabbage with Smoked Sausage

1 head cabbage
¼ pound HILLSHIRE FARM® Bacon, sliced
Salt and black pepper to taste
1 onion, finely chopped
½ cup white wine
½ cup beef broth
1 pound HILLSHIRE FARM® Smoked Sausage, cut into ¼-inch slices

Preheat oven to 350°F.

Clean and quarter cabbage; soak in salted water. Line large casserole with Bacon; add cabbage. Season cabbage with salt and pepper; sprinkle with onion. Pour wine and beef broth over cabbage; top with Smoked Sausage. Bake, covered, 1 hour or until cooked through.

Makes 4 servings

Beef Mole Tamale Pie

Potato-Crusted Meat Loaf

1 large yellow onion
1 large green bell pepper
1 large red bell pepper
3 large cloves garlic
1 pound lean ground beef
1 pound ground veal
¼ cup egg substitute *or* 1 large
   egg, beaten
½ cup bottled chili sauce
1 cup seasoned dry bread
   crumbs, divided

1½ cups (6 ounces) shredded
   ALPINE LACE® Fat Free
   Pasteurized Process Skim
   Milk Cheese Product—For
   Cheddar Lovers, divided
½ teaspoon ground black pepper
1 pound russet baking potatoes,
   peeled, cooked, kept hot
¼ cup minced chives
2 tablespoons unsalted butter
   substitute, melted

1. Preheat the broiler. Place the onion, bell peppers and garlic cloves on a baking sheet. Broil 3 inches from heat for 7 minutes or until blackened, turning frequently. Transfer to a paper bag, close tightly and let stand 15 minutes or until soft. Scrap off outside skins. Chop the onion and garlic; seed and chop the peppers. (You will have about 2 cups vegetables.)

2. Preheat the oven to 350°F and spray a 13×9×3-inch baking dish with nonstick cooking spray. In a large bowl, mix the beef, veal, vegetables, egg substitute (or the whole egg), chili sauce, bread crumbs, the ½ cup of the cheese and the black pepper. Mix with your hands until well combined. Transfer to the baking dish and pat into a 12×7-inch loaf, mounding it slightly in the center.

3. In a small bowl, with an electric mixer set on medium-high, whip the hot potatoes with the 1 cup of cheese, the chives and the butter until fluffy. Pipe or spoon on top and sides of the loaf. Bake for 1 hour or until a meat thermometer inserted into the center of the meat loaf registers 145°F. Let stand for 10 minutes, then serve. *Makes 12 servings*

Nutrients per Serving: Calories 277, Total Fat 10 g, Cholesterol 80 mg

Fix-It-Fast Corned Beef & Cabbage

1 small head cabbage (about
      1½ pounds), cored and cut into
      6 wedges
1 can (12 ounces) corned beef,
      sliced, *or* ½ pound sliced deli
      corned beef
1 can (14 ounces) sliced carrots,
      drained
1 can (16 ounces) sliced potatoes,
      drained
1⅓ cups FRENCH'S® French Fried
      Onions, divided
1 can (10¾ ounces) condensed
      cream of celery soup
¾ cup water

Preheat oven to 375°F. Arrange cabbage wedges and corned beef slices alternately down center of 13×9-inch baking dish. Place carrots, potatoes and *⅔ cup* French Fried Onions along sides of dish. In small bowl, combine soup and water; pour over meat and vegetables. Bake, covered, at 375°F for 40 minutes or until cabbage is tender. Top with remaining *⅔ cup* onions; bake, uncovered, 3 minutes or until onions are golden brown.

Makes 4 to 6 servings

Lean Picadillo Pie

1½ pounds lean ground pork
 ½ cup *each* chopped onion and green
      bell pepper
 1 clove garlic, minced
 1 can (14½ ounces) whole tomatoes,
      undrained, cut up
 ¾ cup chopped dried apricots or
      raisins
12 pimiento-stuffed green olives,
      sliced
 3 tablespoons chili powder
 2 tablespoons chopped almonds
 2 cans (14½ ounces each) chicken
      broth
 2 cups cornmeal

Heat large nonstick skillet over medium heat; cook and stir pork, onion, green pepper and garlic 5 minutes or until pork is lightly browned. Pour off any drippings. Stir in tomatoes, dried apricots, olives, chili powder and almonds. Cover and simmer 10 minutes. Bring chicken broth to a boil in large saucepan. Gradually stir in cornmeal; mix well. Spoon cornmeal mixture into 13×9-inch baking dish sprayed with nonstick cooking spray. Top with pork mixture. Cover with foil. Bake at 350°F for 30 minutes. Cut into squares to serve.   *Makes 12 servings*

Prep Time: 20 minutes
Cook Time: 30 minutes

Favorite recipe from **National Pork Producers Council**

Mexicali Cornbread Casserole

2½ cups frozen mixed vegetables, thawed
1½ cups cubed HILLSHIRE FARM® Ham
1 package (10 ounces) cornbread stuffing mix
2 cups milk
3 eggs, lightly beaten
   Salt and black pepper to taste
½ cup (2 ounces) shredded taco-flavored cheese

Preheat oven to 375°F.

Combine mixed vegetables, Ham and stuffing mix in small casserole; set aside. Combine milk, eggs, salt and pepper in medium bowl; pour over ham mixture. Bake, covered, 45 minutes. Top with cheese; bake, uncovered, 3 minutes or until cheese is melted.

Makes 4 servings

To make bread crumbs, place slices of bread on baking sheet and bake at 300°F until dry. Let cool and crumble into fine pieces.

Reuben Casserole

1 can (10¾ ounces) condensed cream of mushroom soup, undiluted
¾ cup milk
¼ cup chopped onion
½ tablespoon mustard
1 can (16 ounces) sauerkraut, rinsed and drained
1 package (8 ounces) uncooked noodles
1 pound HILLSHIRE FARM® Polska Kielbasa, cut into ½-inch pieces
1 cup (4 ounces) shredded Swiss cheese
½ cup bread crumbs
2 tablespoons butter, melted

Preheat oven to 350°F.

Grease 13×9-inch baking pan. Combine soup, milk, onion and mustard in medium bowl. Spread sauerkraut onto bottom of prepared pan, pressing firmly. Add noodles. Spoon soup mixture evenly over noodles; cover with Polska Kielbasa. Top with cheese. Combine bread crumbs and butter in small bowl; sprinkle over cheese. Cover tightly. Bake 1 hour or until noodles are tender.

Makes 6 servings

Mexicali Cornbread Casserole

Zesty Italian Stuffed Peppers

3 bell peppers (green, red or yellow)
1 pound ground beef
1 jar (14 ounces) spaghetti sauce
1⅓ cups FRENCH'S® French Fried
    Onions, divided
2 tablespoons FRANK'S® Original
    REDHOT® Cayenne Pepper Sauce
½ cup uncooked instant rice
¼ cup sliced ripe olives
1 cup (4 ounces) shredded
    mozzarella cheese

Preheat oven to 400°F. Cut bell peppers in half lengthwise through stems; discard seeds. Place pepper halves, cut side up, in 2-quart shallow baking dish; set aside.

Place beef in large microwavable bowl. Microwave on HIGH 5 minutes or until meat is browned, stirring once. Drain. Stir in spaghetti sauce, ⅔ cup French Fried Onions, RedHot® sauce, rice and olives. Spoon evenly into bell pepper halves.

Cover; bake 35 minutes or until bell peppers are tender. Uncover; sprinkle with cheese and remaining ⅔ cup onions. Bake 1 minute or until onions are golden.   *Makes 6 servings*

Prep Time: 10 minutes
Cook Time: 36 minutes

Fiesta Corn Casserole

1 tablespoon butter
3 cups cornflakes, divided
1 pound ground beef
1 can (8 ounces) tomato sauce
1 package (1.0 ounce) LAWRY'S®
    Taco Spices & Seasonings
½ teaspoon LAWRY'S® Seasoned Salt
1 can (17 ounces) whole kernel corn,
    drained (reserve ¼ cup liquid)
2 cups (8 ounces) shredded cheddar
    cheese

In large skillet, melt butter. Add 2 cups cornflakes; mix well. Remove buttered cornflakes and set aside. Wipe skillet clean. In same skillet, brown ground beef over medium-high heat until crumbly; drain fat. Add tomato sauce, Taco Spices & Seasonings, Seasoned Salt and ¼ cup corn liquid; mix well. In 1½-quart casserole, layer half buttered corn flakes, corn, meat mixture and cheese; repeat layers. Sprinkle remaining 1 cup crushed cornflakes over top in diagonal strips. Bake in 350°F oven 15 to 20 minutes until heated through.   *Makes 4 to 6 servings*

Serving Suggestion: Serve with sliced tomatoes, cucumbers and fresh fruit.

Hint: May use 2 cups broken taco shell pieces and 1 cup crushed taco shells.

Zesty Italian Stuffed Pepper

Zucchini Lasagna

1½ pounds ground beef
¾ pound sweet Italian sausage, casing removed
3 tablespoons FILIPPO BERIO® Olive Oil
1½ cups coarsely chopped mushrooms
1 large onion, chopped
1 large clove garlic, minced
1 can (14½ ounces) tomatoes, chopped, undrained
1 jar (15 ounces) marinara sauce
1 teaspoon salt
1 teaspoon dried basil leaves, crushed
½ teaspoon Italian herb seasoning
1 container (24 ounces) ricotta cheese
1 package (8 ounces) mozzarella cheese, cubed, divided
¼ cup chopped Italian parsley
2 eggs, beaten
6 unpeeled zucchini, cut lengthwise into thin slices about 8 inches long

Cook beef and sausage in hot oil in large skillet over medium-high heat until meats are no longer pink. Add mushrooms, onion and garlic. Cook several minutes, stirring frequently. Add tomatoes with juice, marinara sauce, salt, basil and Italian seasoning. Combine ricotta, ¾ of the mozzarella, parsley and eggs in medium bowl. Spoon 1 cup of the sauce onto bottom of 13×9-inch baking dish. Top with ⅓ of the zucchini, ⅓ of the cheese mixture and then 1 cup of the sauce. Repeat layers twice, ending with sauce. Cover with foil. Bake at 350°F for 45 minutes. Sprinkle with remaining mozzarella. Bake, uncovered, 10 minutes more or until cheese melts. Let stand 10 minutes before cutting. Heat remaining sauce and serve with lasagna. *Makes 8 servings*

Classic Hamburger Casserole

1 pound ground beef
1 package (9 ounces) frozen cut green beans, thawed and drained
1 can (10¾ ounces) condensed tomato soup
¼ cup water
½ teaspoon seasoned salt
⅛ teaspoon pepper
2 cups hot mashed potatoes
1⅓ cups FRENCH'S® French Fried Onions, divided
½ cup (2 ounces) shredded Cheddar cheese

Preheat oven to 350°F. In medium skillet, brown ground beef; drain. Stir in green beans, soup, water and seasonings; pour into 1½-quart casserole. In medium bowl, combine mashed potatoes and ⅔ cup French Fried Onions. Spoon potato mixture in mounds around edge of casserole. Bake, uncovered, at 350°F for 25 minutes or until heated through. Top potatoes with cheese and remaining ⅔ cup onions; bake, uncovered, 5 minutes or until onions are golden brown.
Makes 4 to 6 servings

Country Classic

Stuffed Pasta Shells

8 large uncooked manicotti
   shells
2 tablespoons olive oil
¼ cup chopped onion
1 teaspoon minced garlic
1 (10-ounce) package frozen
   spinach, thawed and
   squeezed dry
6 tablespoons butter, divided
1 pound BOB EVANS® Original
   Recipe or Italian Roll
   Sausage
9 tablespoons grated Parmesan
   cheese, divided

1 cup plus 2 tablespoons milk,
   divided
2 eggs, lightly beaten
½ teaspoon dried oregano leaves
4 tablespoons all-purpose flour
1 cup whipping cream
   Salt and black pepper to taste
1 (26- to 28-ounce) jar tomato-
   based spaghetti sauce
2 tablespoons butter, cut in
   small pieces

Place manicotti shells in salted boiling water and cook until tender. Drain
and set aside to cool. Heat oil in large skillet. Add onion and garlic; cook
over low heat until tender. Add spinach; cook until liquid has evaporated.
Transfer mixture to medium bowl. Add 2 tablespoons butter to same skillet;
crumble sausage into skillet and cook until lightly browned. Stir sausage into
spinach mixture. Add 5 tablespoons cheese, 2 tablespoons milk, eggs and
oregano; mix well. Transfer mixture to pastry bag and pipe into manicotti
shells.

To prepare sauce, melt 4 tablespoons butter in medium saucepan. Stir in
flour, a little at a time, mixing well. Add remaining 1 cup milk and cream all
at once, whisking constantly until flour is incorporated. Bring to a boil over
high heat. Reduce heat to low; cook and stir 2 to 3 minutes until sauce is
thick enough to coat wires of whisk. Remove from heat and season with salt
and pepper.

Preheat oven to 375°F. Pour just enough spaghetti sauce on bottom of 13×9-
inch glass baking dish to coat surface. Arrange stuffed manicotti over sauce
in single layer. Pour cream sauce over manicotti; top with the remaining
spaghetti sauce and remaining 4 tablespoons cheese. Dot with 2 tablespoons
cut-up butter. Bake 20 minutes or until sauce is bubbling. Place dish under
hot broiler and cook just until top is browned. *Makes 4 servings*

Baked Pork Fajitas Mexicana

2 medium red or green peppers, cut
    into strips
1 medium onion, sliced
2 tablespoons oil
1 tablespoon lemon or lime juice
8 boneless pork chops (½ inch thick)
1 envelope SHAKE 'N BAKE®
    Seasoned Coating Mix Original
    Pork
    Flour tortillas, warmed

MIX peppers, onion, oil and lemon
juice in 13×9-inch baking pan until
well mixed.

COAT chops with coating mix as
directed on package. Place on pepper
mixture.

BAKE at 425°F for 20 minutes or until
chops are cooked through. Cut chops
into slices. Fill tortillas with sliced pork
and pepper mixture *or* serve whole
chops and vegetables over rice.

Makes 8 servings

Prep Time: 10 minutes
Bake Time: 20 minutes

Layered Mexicali Casserole

1 pound ground beef
1 (16-ounce) can ROSARITA® Refried
    Beans
1 (15-ounce) can HUNT'S® Ready
    Tomato Sauces Chunky Special
1 (1-ounce) package taco seasoning
    mix
1 teaspoon garlic salt
    WESSON® No-Stick Cooking Spray
6 (8-inch) flour tortillas
1 (14½-ounce) can HUNT'S® Choice-
    Cut Tomatoes, drained
¾ cup sliced green onions
1 (4-ounce) can diced green chiles
1 (2¼-ounce) can sliced ripe olives,
    drained
4 cups (16 ounces) shredded
    Cheddar cheese
    Sour cream (optional)
    Avocado slices (optional)

Preheat oven to 350°F. In large skillet,
brown ground beef; drain. Stir in beans,
tomato sauce, taco seasoning, and
garlic salt. Bring to a boil; reduce heat
and simmer 5 minutes. In 13×9×2-inch
baking dish, lightly sprayed with
cooking spray, place 2 tortillas side by
side on bottom of dish. Spread ⅓ of
meat mixture over tortillas and sprinkle
with ⅓ of each of tomatoes, onions,
chiles, olives, and cheese. Repeat layers
twice, ending with cheese.

Bake for 40 minutes. Let stand 10
minutes before serving. Garnish each
serving with sour cream and an
avocado slice, if desired.

Makes 8 to 10 servings

Baked Pork Fajitas Mexicana

Beef Enchiladas

Red Chili Sauce (recipe follows)
1½ pounds lean boneless beef chuck,
    cut into 1-inch cubes
½ teaspoon salt
2 tablespoons vegetable oil
½ cup finely chopped white onion
¾ cup beef broth
¼ cup raisins
1 clove garlic, minced
½ teaspoon ground cloves
¼ teaspoon anise seeds, crushed
12 corn tortillas (6-inch diameter)
1 cup (4 ounces) shredded mild
    Cheddar cheese
¾ cup sour cream
⅓ cup sliced pitted ripe olives
    Basil sprig and tomato wedge for
    garnish

1. Prepare Red Chili Sauce.

2. Sprinkle beef with salt. Brown half of beef in hot oil in large skillet over medium-high heat 10 to 12 minutes, turning frequently. Remove with slotted spoon to plate. Repeat with remaining beef.

3. Reduce heat to medium. Add onion; cook and stir 4 minutes or until onion is softened. Return beef to skillet. Stir in broth, raisins, garlic, cloves, anise seeds and ¼ cup Red Chili Sauce. Bring to a boil over medium-high heat. Reduce heat to low. Cover and simmer 1½ to 2 hours until beef is very tender. Using 2 forks, pull beef into coarse shreds in skillet. Remove from heat.

4. Preheat oven to 375°F. Heat remaining Red Chili Sauce in medium skillet over medium heat until hot; remove from heat.

5. Dip 1 tortilla in sauce with tongs a few seconds or until limp. Remove, draining off excess sauce. Spread about 3 tablespoons meat filling down center of tortilla. Roll up; place on sauce in 13×9-inch baking dish. Repeat with remaining tortillas, sauce and meat filling. Pour remaining sauce over enchiladas.

6. Sprinkle cheese over top. Bake 25 minutes or until bubbly and cheese is melted. To serve, spoon sour cream down center of enchiladas. Sprinkle with olives. Garnish, if desired.

Makes 4 to 6 servings

Red Chili Sauce

3 ounces dried ancho chilies
    (about 5), toasted, seeded,
    deveined, rinsed
2½ cups boiling water
2 tablespoons vegetable oil
2 tablespoons tomato paste
1 clove garlic, minced
½ teaspoon salt
½ teaspoon dried oregano leaves,
    crushed
¼ teaspoon ground cumin
¼ teaspoon ground coriander

1. Place chilies in medium bowl; cover with boiling water. Let stand 1 hour.

2. Place chilies along with soaking water in blender; process until smooth.

3. Pour into 2-quart saucepan; whisk in remaining ingredients. Bring to a boil over medium-high heat. Reduce heat to very low. Cover and simmer 10 minutes, stirring occasionally.

Makes about 2½ cups

Beef Enchiladas

Bratwurst Skillet

**1 pound bratwurst links, cut into
½-inch slices
1½ cups green bell pepper strips
1½ cups red bell pepper strips
1½ cups sliced onions
1 teaspoon paprika
1 teaspoon caraway seeds**

1. Heat large skillet over medium heat until hot. Add bratwurst; cover and cook about 5 minutes or until browned and no longer pink in center. Transfer bratwurst to plate. Cover and keep warm.

2. Drain all but 1 tablespoon drippings from skillet. Add bell peppers, onions, paprika and caraway seeds. Cook and stir about 5 minutes or until vegetables are tender.

3. Combine bratwurst and vegetables. Serve immediately.

Makes 4 servings

Cutting Corners: To make this even speedier, purchase a packaged stir-fry pepper and onion mix and use in place of the bell peppers and onions.

Prep and Cook Time: 18 minutes

Creamy Beef and Vegetable Casserole

**1 pound lean ground beef
1 small onion, chopped
1 bag (16 ounces) BIRDS EYE® frozen Farm Fresh Mixtures Broccoli, Corn & Red Peppers
1 can (10¾ ounces) cream of mushroom soup**

● In medium skillet, brown beef and onion; drain excess fat.

● Meanwhile, in large saucepan, cook vegetables according to package directions; drain.

● Stir in beef mixture and soup. Cook over medium heat until heated through.

Makes 4 servings

Serving Suggestion: Serve over rice and sprinkle with ½ cup shredded Cheddar cheese.

Prep Time: 5 minutes
Cook Time: 10 to 15 minutes

Bratwurst Skillet

Lightened Up

Smoked Sausage Skillet Dinner

2¼ cups (9 ounces) elbow
    macaroni, uncooked
1 (14-ounce) package HEALTHY
    CHOICE® Low Fat Smoked
    Sausage
1 cup chopped onion
½ cup sliced celery
½ cup chopped green bell pepper

1½ teaspoons vegetable oil
1 (14½-ounce) can no-salt-
    added stewed tomatoes,
    undrained and chopped
1 teaspoon chili powder
¼ teaspoon ground black pepper
½ cup HEALTHY CHOICE® Fat
    Free Cheddar Shreds

Cook macaroni according to package directions, omitting salt and fat. Drain well and set aside.

Cut sausage into ¼-inch-thick slices. Cook sausage, onion, celery and bell pepper in oil in large, deep nonstick skillet over medium heat 8 minutes or until sausage is lightly browned and vegetables are tender, stirring occasionally.

Add macaroni, tomatoes, chili powder and ground pepper; mix well. Cook, uncovered, 4 minutes or until mixture is thoroughly heated, stirring frequently.

Sprinkle Cheddar shreds evenly over sausage mixture; cook, uncovered, until Cheddar shreds soften, stirring occasionally. Serve immediately.

Makes 8 (1-cup) servings

Tip: Be sure to use a large, deep nonstick skillet to prepare this recipe so there will be enough room to adequately stir the ingredients. Also, if other brands of sausage or cheese are used, compare nutrition labels to make sure they feature similar low levels of fat, cholesterol and sodium.

Nutrients per Serving: Calories 224, Total Fat 3 g, Cholesterol 28 mg, Sodium 578 mg

Cajun Pork Skillet Dinner

1 tablespoon vegetable oil
4 rib-cut pork chops* (about
1 pound), cut ³/₄ inch thick
1 jar (16 ounces) chunky medium
salsa
1¹/₃ cups FRENCH'S® French Fried
Onions, divided
¹/₂ teaspoon dried thyme leaves
Cooked white rice (optional)

*Or, substitute 1 pound boneless skinless chicken breasts for pork chops.

Heat oil in large nonstick skillet. Add pork chops; cook about 5 minutes or until browned on both sides.

Stir in salsa, *²/₃ cup* French Fried Onions and thyme. Bring to a boil over high heat. Reduce heat to medium-low. Cover; cook 10 minutes or until pork is no longer pink near bone, stirring occasionally. Sprinkle remaining *²/₃ cup* onions over pork. Serve with rice, if desired.   *Makes 4 servings*

Tip: For a Mediterranean flare, substitute ¹/₂ teaspoon oregano for ¹/₂ teaspoon thyme.

Prep Time: 5 minutes
Cook Time: 15 minutes

Ham Paella with Sun-Dried Tomatoes and Pine Nuts

¹/₄ cup extra-virgin olive oil
2 pounds HILLSHIRE FARM® Ham,
sliced into 2×¹/₂-inch strips
1 onion, chopped
12 sun-dried tomatoes packed in olive
oil
3 tablespoons pine nuts
4 cloves garlic, minced
2 cups uncooked rice
4 cups chicken broth, heated
¹/₂ cup chopped parsley
¹/₄ cup sliced pitted green olives
1 teaspoon ground cumin
Salt and freshly ground black
pepper to taste

Heat oil in medium saucepan over medium-high heat. Brown Ham in hot oil, about 30 seconds on each side. Remove ham from saucepan; set aside. Add onion to saucepan; reduce heat to medium and sauté 10 minutes. Add tomatoes, pine nuts and garlic; sauté 5 minutes. Add rice; sauté, stirring constantly, 3 to 4 minutes. Stir in chicken broth, parsley, olives, cumin and ham. Season with salt and pepper. Reduce heat to low; simmer, covered, 30 to 40 minutes or until rice is tender and liquid is absorbed.

Makes 6 servings

Hearty Hot Dish

⅓ cup honey
¼ cup spicy brown mustard
¼ cup vegetable oil
1 tablespoon soy sauce
2 cloves garlic, minced
1 teaspoon ground ginger
1 pound HILLSHIRE FARM® Beef
    Smoked Sausage,* sliced
2 onions, cut into quarters
1 cup chopped carrots
1 cup chopped celery
1 cup sliced mushrooms

*Or use any variety Hillshire Farm® Smoked Sausage.

Combine honey, mustard, oil, soy sauce, garlic and ginger in large bowl; blend thoroughly. Add Smoked Sausage, onions, carrots, celery and mushrooms. Sauté sausage mixture in large skillet over medium-high heat until sausage is lightly browned.   *Makes 4 to 6 servings*

To clean mushrooms,

wipe with a damp

paper towel. Never

soak mushrooms because

they will absorb liquids

and become soggy.

Pork Curry

2 tablespoons vegetable oil, divided
1 pound boneless pork tenderloin,
    cut into ¾-inch cubes
1 large onion, cut in half lengthwise
    and thinly sliced
1 small carrot, shredded
1 clove garlic, minced
1 tablespoon curry powder
1 package (8 ounces) frozen sugar
    snap peas
1 Granny Smith or McIntosh apple,
    cut into thin wedges
1 can (6 ounces) frozen apple juice
    concentrate, thawed
2 tablespoons FRANK'S® Original
    REDHOT® Cayenne Pepper Sauce
¼ cup nonfat sour cream
    Cooked white rice (optional)

1. Heat 1 tablespoon oil in large nonstick skillet over medium-high heat. Add pork; cook and stir 5 minutes or until browned. Transfer to platter; set aside. Heat remaining 1 tablespoon oil in same skillet. Add onion, carrot and garlic; cook and stir until tender. Stir in curry powder; cook 1 minute.

2. Return pork to skillet; stir in sugar snap peas, apple, juice and RedHot® sauce. Bring to a boil. Reduce heat to low; cook, uncovered, 5 minutes or until pork is no longer pink and sugar snap peas and apple are tender. Stir in sour cream. Serve with rice, if desired.
          Makes 4 servings

Prep Time: 20 minutes
Cook Time: 20 minutes

Hearty Hot Dish

Beefy Bean & Walnut Stir-Fry

1 teaspoon vegetable oil
3 cloves garlic, minced
1 pound lean ground beef or ground turkey
1 bag (16 ounces) BIRDS EYE® frozen Cut Green Beans, thawed
1 teaspoon salt
½ cup walnut pieces

● In large skillet, heat oil and garlic over medium heat about 30 seconds.

● Add beef and beans; sprinkle with salt. Mix well.

● Cook 5 minutes or until beef is well browned, stirring occasionally.

● Stir in walnuts; cook 2 minutes more.
Makes 4 servings

Serving Suggestion: Serve over hot cooked egg noodles or rice.

Prep Time: 5 minutes
Cook Time: 7 to 10 minutes

Tofu, made from ground, cooked soybeans, is a great source of protein that's cholesterol-free.

Hunan Pork & Tofu Stir-Fry

1 block (14 to 16 ounces) firm tofu, drained
½ pound ground pork
1 tablespoon dry sherry
1 teaspoon minced fresh ginger root
1 clove garlic, minced
½ cup chicken broth
1 tablespoon cornstarch
3 tablespoons KIKKOMAN® Soy Sauce
1 tablespoon vinegar
½ teaspoon crushed red pepper
1 tablespoon vegetable oil
1 onion, cut into ¾-inch pieces
1 green bell pepper, cut into ¾-inch pieces

Cut tofu into ½-inch cubes; drain well on paper towels. Meanwhile, combine pork, sherry, ginger and garlic; let stand 10 minutes. Blend chicken broth, cornstarch, soy sauce, vinegar and crushed red pepper; set aside. Heat wok or large skillet over medium-high heat; add pork. Cook, stirring to separate pork, about 3 minutes, or until lightly browned; remove. Heat oil in same pan. Add onion and bell pepper; stir-fry 4 minutes. Add pork and soy sauce mixture. Cook and stir until mixture boils and thickens. Gently fold in tofu; heat through.   *Makes 4 servings*

Beefy Bean & Walnut Stir-Fry

Country Classic

Sweet and Sour Pork

³/₄ pound boneless pork
1 teaspoon vegetable oil
1 bag (16 ounces) BIRDS EYE®
   frozen Farm Fresh Mixtures
   Pepper Stir Fry vegetables

1 tablespoon water
1 jar (14 ounces) sweet and sour
   sauce
1 can (8 ounces) pineapple
   chunks, drained

- Cut pork into thin strips.

- In large skillet, heat oil over medium-high heat.

- Add pork; stir-fry until pork is browned.

- Add vegetables and water; cover and cook over medium heat 5 to 7 minutes or until vegetables are crisp-tender.

- Uncover; stir in sweet and sour sauce and pineapple. Cook until heated through. *Makes 4 servings*

Serving Suggestion: Serve over hot cooked rice.

Prep Time: 5 minutes
Cook Time: 15 to 18 minutes

Spicy Sausage Stir-Fry

2 tablespoons vegetable oil
2 cups broccoli florets
2 cups sliced mushrooms
1 green bell pepper, cut into strips
2 tablespoons soy sauce
1 (9-ounce) HILLSHIRE FARM®
   Summer Sausage, cut into
   matchstick-size pieces
4 cups cooked rice
3 large eggs, beaten
¹/₂ to ³/₄ teaspoon red pepper flakes

Heat oil in large deep skillet or wok over high heat. Add broccoli, mushrooms and bell pepper; stir-fry 1 minute. Add soy sauce and 2 tablespoons water; stir-fry 6 minutes or until vegetables are crisp-tender. Add Summer Sausage; stir-fry 2 minutes. Add rice; stir-fry 1 minute or until heated through. Combine eggs and pepper flakes in small bowl. Add egg mixture to skillet; stir-fry 3 minutes or until eggs are set. *Makes 6 servings*

Sweet and Sour Pork

Garlic Lamb and Eggplant Stir-Fry

½ pound boneless lamb
1 tablespoon KIKKOMAN® Stir-Fry
    Sauce
1½ teaspoons minced garlic, divided
1 pound eggplant, trimmed
4 tablespoons vegetable oil, divided
⅛ teaspoon salt
1 onion, thinly sliced
1 red bell pepper, cut into
    matchsticks
1 crookneck squash, cut into
    matchsticks
⅓ cup KIKKOMAN® Stir-Fry Sauce
⅛ teaspoon crushed red pepper

Cut lamb into thin strips. Coat lamb in medium bowl with mixture of 1 tablespoon stir-fry sauce and ½ teaspoon garlic; let stand 30 minutes. Meanwhile, peel eggplant lengthwise to form stripes; then cut into matchsticks. Heat 1 tablespoon oil in hot wok or large skillet over high heat. Add lamb and stir-fry 1 minute; remove. Heat 2 tablespoons oil in same pan; reduce heat to medium-high. Add remaining 1 teaspoon garlic; stir-fry 10 seconds. Add eggplant and salt; stir-fry 6 minutes. Push eggplant to edge of pan; add remaining 1 tablespoon oil, onion, bell pepper and squash; stir-fry with eggplant 5 minutes. Add ⅓ cup stir-fry sauce and crushed red pepper; cook, stirring constantly, 2 minutes longer. Stir in lamb; heat through.

Makes 4 servings

Meat and Potato Stir-Fry

1 tablespoon vegetable oil
1 large baking potato, peeled and cut
    into ½-inch cubes
2 medium carrots, peeled and thinly
    sliced
1 medium onion, halved and sliced
⅔ cup beef broth
1 teaspoon salt, divided
1 pound lean ground round
1 large clove garlic, minced
1 tablespoon dried parsley flakes
1 teaspoon paprika
½ teaspoon ground cinnamon
½ teaspoon ground cumin
¼ teaspoon pepper

1. Heat oil in wok or large skillet over medium-high heat until hot. Add potato, carrots and onion; cook and stir 3 minutes. Stir in broth and ½ teaspoon salt. Reduce heat to medium. Cover and cook 6 to 7 minutes or until potato is tender, stirring once or twice. Remove vegetables from wok; set aside. Wipe out wok with paper towel.

2. Heat wok over medium-high heat until hot. Add ground beef and garlic; stir-fry 3 minutes or until meat is no longer pink. Add parsley, paprika, cinnamon, cumin, remaining ½ teaspoon salt and pepper; cook and stir 1 minute. Add vegetables; heat through.

Makes 4 servings

Serving Suggestion: Serve Meat and Potato Stir-Fry as a filling for pita bread.

Prep and Cook Time: 25 minutes

Szechuan Pork & Vegetables

4 butterflied pork loin chops, ½ inch thick (1 to 1¼ pounds)
¼ cup plus 1 tablespoon stir-fry sauce, divided
¾ teaspoon bottled minced ginger _or_ ½ teaspoon ground ginger
1 package (16 ounces) frozen Oriental-style vegetables, thawed
1 can (5 ounces) crisp chow mein noodles
2 tablespoons chopped green onion

1. Heat large, deep nonstick skillet over medium heat until hot. Add pork. Spoon 1 tablespoon stir-fry sauce over pork; sprinkle with ginger. Cook 3 minutes. Turn pork; cook 3 minutes. Transfer chops to plate; set aside.

2. Add vegetables and remaining ¼ cup stir-fry sauce to skillet. Cook over medium-low heat 3 minutes; add pork. Cook 3 minutes or until pork is no longer pink in center, stirring vegetables and turning chops once.

3. While pork is cooking, arrange chow mein noodles around edges of 4 serving plates. Transfer chops to plates. Top noodles with vegetable mixture. Sprinkle with green onion.

Makes 4 servings

Prep and Cook Time: 12 minutes

Lamb Firepot

1 pound boneless lamb sirloin chops or beef sirloin steak, about ½ inch thick
3 tablespoons dry sherry, divided
2½ tablespoons KIKKOMAN® Soy Sauce, divided
2 teaspoons minced fresh ginger root
1 clove garlic, minced
2 cans (about 14 ounces each) ⅓-less-salt chicken broth
1 pound bok choy cabbage
8 ounces firm tofu, drained and cut into 1-inch cubes
6 green onions and tops, cut into 1½-inch lengths
¼ pound fresh mushrooms, sliced
4 ounces vermicelli, cooked and drained

Trim excess fat from lamb and cut across grain into thin slices. Combine 1 tablespoon sherry, 1½ tablespoons soy sauce, ginger and garlic in small bowl; stir in lamb. Let stand 15 minutes. Meanwhile, combine chicken broth, remaining 2 tablespoons sherry and 1 tablespoon soy sauce in deep electric skillet or electric wok; bring to boil. Reduce heat; keep broth mixture hot. Cut bok choy stems and leaves crosswise into ½-inch slices. Arrange with tofu, green onions, mushrooms and vermicelli on large serving platter. Using chopsticks or tongs, let individuals select and add lamb, vegetables and vermicelli to hot broth. Cook lamb and vegetables to desired degree of doneness, keeping broth mixture hot. Serve in individual bowls. When all foods are cooked, serve broth as soup. _Makes 4 to 6 servings_

Wisconsin Sausage Soup

½ cup butter
1 onion, chopped
1 carrot, chopped
1 teaspoon minced garlic
1 cup all-purpose flour
2 cups chicken broth
2 cups milk
¾ cup beer
1 teaspoon Worcestershire sauce
½ teaspoon salt
½ teaspoon dry mustard
1 bay leaf
7 ounces Cheddar cheese, shredded
3 ounces Swiss cheese, shredded
½ pound HILLSHIRE FARM® Smoked Sausage

Melt butter in medium saucepan over medium heat. Add onion, carrot and garlic; sauté until softened. Add flour; cook 5 minutes, stirring often. Add chicken broth, milk, beer, Worcestershire sauce, salt, mustard and bay leaf. Reduce heat to low; cook until soup has thickened, whisking often.

Slowly whisk cheeses into soup until combined and smooth. Cut Smoked Sausage lengthwise into quarters, then slice into ½-inch pieces. Sauté sausage in small skillet over medium-high heat until heated through. Blot excess grease with paper towels; add to soup. Remove bay leaf; serve soup hot.

Makes 8 to 10 servings

Italian Sausage Soup

2 boxes (10 ounces each) BIRDS EYE® frozen Italian Style Vegetables
2 cans (14 ounces each) beef broth
1 pound cooked Italian sausage, cubed
1 can (8 ounces) tomato sauce

● In large saucepan, place vegetables and broth; bring to boil over high heat. Reduce heat to medium; cover and simmer 7 to 10 minutes or until vegetables are crisp-tender.

● Stir in cooked sausage and tomato sauce; cook until heated through.

Makes 4 servings

Prep Time: 2 minutes
Cook Time: 10 to 12 minutes

Wisconsin Sausage Soup

Taco Soup

1 pound BOB EVANS® Original
    Recipe or Zesty Hot Roll Sausage
1½ tablespoons olive oil
 ½ small Spanish onion, diced
 1 jalapeño pepper, seeded and diced
1½ cups beef broth
 1 cup peeled, seeded, diced fresh or
    canned tomatoes
 1 cup vegetable juice
 ½ tablespoon ground cumin
 ½ tablespoon chili powder
 ¼ teaspoon salt
 ⅓ cup shredded Cheddar cheese
 12 tortilla chips, broken into pieces

Crumble and cook sausage in olive oil in Dutch oven until no longer pink but not yet browned. Add onion and pepper; cook until onion is tender. Add remaining ingredients except cheese and chips; bring to a boil over high heat. Reduce heat to low and simmer, uncovered, 15 minutes. Ladle soup into bowls; garnish with cheese and chips. Refrigerate leftovers.
Makes 6 servings

*Chili peppers can sting
and irritate the skin.
Wash your hands after
handling peppers and
do not touch your eyes.*

Texas Beef Stew

1 pound lean ground beef
1 small onion, chopped
1 can (28 ounces) crushed tomatoes
    with roasted garlic
1½ cups BIRDS EYE® frozen Farm Fresh
    Mixtures Broccoli, Cauliflower &
    Carrots
1 can (14½ ounces) whole new
    potatoes, halved
1 cup BIRDS EYE® frozen Sweet Corn
1 can (4½ ounces) chopped green
    chilies, drained
½ cup water

● In large saucepan, cook beef and onion over medium-high heat until beef is well browned, stirring occasionally.

● Stir in tomatoes, vegetables, potatoes with liquid, corn, chilies and water; bring to boil.

● Reduce heat to medium-low; cover and simmer 5 minutes or until heated through.
Makes 4 servings

Serving Suggestion: Serve over rice and with warm crusty bread.

Prep Time: 5 minutes
Cook Time: 15 minutes

Taco Soup

Beef Bourguignon

1 boneless beef sirloin steak, ½ inch thick, trimmed, cut into ½-inch pieces (about 3 pounds)
½ cup all-purpose flour
4 slices bacon, diced
3 cups Burgundy wine or beef broth
2 medium carrots, diced
1 teaspoon dried marjoram leaves, crushed
½ teaspoon dried thyme leaves, crushed
½ teaspoon salt
   Black pepper to taste
1 bay leaf
2 tablespoons vegetable oil
20 to 24 fresh pearl onions
8 small new red potatoes, cut into quarters
8 to 10 mushrooms, sliced
3 cloves garlic, minced

Coat beef with flour, shaking off excess. Set aside.

Cook and stir bacon in 5-quart Dutch oven over medium-high heat until partially cooked. Brown half of beef with bacon in Dutch oven over medium-high heat. Remove with slotted spoon; set aside. Brown remaining beef. Pour off drippings. Return beef and bacon to Dutch oven.

Stir in wine, carrots, marjoram, thyme, salt, pepper and bay leaf. Bring to a boil over high heat. Reduce heat to low. Cover and simmer 10 minutes.

Meanwhile, heat oil in large saucepan over medium-high heat. Cook and stir onions, potatoes, mushrooms and garlic about 10 minutes. Add to Dutch oven. Cover and simmer 50 minutes or until meat is fork-tender. Discard bay leaf before serving.

Makes 10 to 12 servings

White Sausage Chili

2 tablespoons vegetable oil
1 pound HILLSHIRE FARM® Smoked Sausage, cut into ½-inch pieces
1 onion, diced
1 can (15 ounces) navy beans, rinsed and drained
1 can (15 ounces) chick-peas, rinsed and drained
1 can (15 ounces) white kernel corn, drained
1 can (about 14 ounces) chicken broth
1 cup cooked wild rice
1 can (4 ounces) diced green chilies, drained
1½ teaspoons ground cumin
¼ teaspoon garlic powder
⅛ teaspoon hot pepper sauce
   Chopped parsley

Heat oil in large saucepan over medium-high heat. Sauté Smoked Sausage and onion until onion is soft and sausage is lightly browned, about 5 minutes. Stir in all remaining ingredients, except parsley. Simmer, covered, 20 minutes. Spoon into 6 individual serving bowls; garnish with parsley. *Makes 6 servings*

Lightened Up

Beef Stew in Red Wine

1½ pounds boneless meat round,
     cut into 1-inch cubes
1½ cups dry red wine
  2 teaspoons olive oil
     Peel of half an orange
  2 large cloves garlic, thinly
     sliced
  1 bay leaf
½ teaspoon dried thyme leaves
⅛ teaspoon pepper
  8 ounces fresh mushrooms,
     quartered

8 sun-dried tomatoes, quartered
1 can (about 14 ounces) fat-free
     reduced-sodium beef broth
6 small potatoes, unpeeled, cut
     into wedges
1 cup baby carrots
1 cup fresh pearl onions, outer
     skins removed
1 tablespoon cornstarch mixed
     with 2 tablespoons water

1. Combine beef, wine, oil, orange peel, garlic, bay leaf, thyme and pepper
in large glass bowl. Refrigerate, covered, at least 2 hours or overnight.

2. Place beef mixture, mushrooms and tomatoes in large nonstick skillet or
Dutch oven. Add enough beef broth to just cover ingredients. Bring to a boil
over high heat. Cover; reduce heat to low. Simmer 1 hour. Add potatoes,
carrots and onions; cover and cook 20 to 25 minutes or until vegetables are
tender and meat is no longer pink. Remove meat and vegetables from skillet
with slotted spoon; cover and set aside. Discard orange peel and bay leaf.

3. Stir cornstarch mixture into skillet with sauce. Increase heat to medium;
cook, stirring until sauce is slightly thickened. Return meat and vegetables to
sauce; heat thoroughly.   *Makes 6 servings*

Nutrients per Serving: Calories 313, Total Fat 6 g, Cholesterol 55 mg, Sodium 304 mg

POTLUCK POULTRY

Chicken & Rice Bake

  1 can (10¾ ounces) condensed
       cream of mushroom soup
1¾ cups water
  ¾ cup uncooked long-grain rice
1½ cups sliced mushrooms
1⅓ cups FRENCH'S® French Fried
       Onions, divided
  4 teaspoons FRENCH'S®
       Worcestershire Sauce, divided
  4 chicken breast halves (about
       2 pounds)
  ½ teaspoon *each* paprika and dried
       thyme leaves

Preheat oven to 375°F. Combine soup, water, rice, mushrooms, ⅔ *cup* French Fried Onions and 2 teaspoons Worcestershire in 3-quart oblong baking dish. Arrange chicken over rice mixture. Brush chicken with remaining Worcestershire and sprinkle with paprika and thyme.

Bake, uncovered, 1 hour or until chicken is no longer pink in center. Top with remaining ⅔ *cup* onions. Bake 3 minutes or until onions are golden.

Makes 4 servings

Tip: Remove skin from chicken before baking, if desired.

Prep Time: 10 minutes
Cook Time: about 1 hour

Chicken & Rice Bake

Sausage and Potato Bake

1 pound small red new potatoes, cut into halves or quarters
1½ cups sliced onions
½ pound baby carrots
2 tablespoons vegetable oil
1 envelope (1¼ ounces) savory herb with garlic flavor dry soup mix
1 pound HILLSHIRE FARM® Gourmet Cooked Sausage—Chicken and Turkey with Apples and Spice, diagonally cut into ⅓-inch slices

Preheat oven to 400°F.

Spray 13×9-inch baking pan with nonstick cooking spray. Combine potatoes, onions, carrots, oil and soup mix in large bowl. Stir until evenly coated.

Place potato mixture into prepared pan; bake, uncovered, 30 minutes. Add Gourmet Sausage to potato mixture; stir well. Return pan to oven; bake 15 to 20 minutes or until potatoes are tender and golden brown.

Makes 5 to 6 servings

Teriyaki Chicken Medley

2 cups cooked white rice (about ¾ cup uncooked)
2 cups (10 ounces) cooked chicken, cut into strips
1⅓ cups FRENCH'S® French Fried Onions, divided
1 package (12 ounces) frozen bell pepper strips, thawed and drained*
1 jar (12 ounces) chicken gravy
3 tablespoons teriyaki sauce

*Or, substitute 2 cups sliced bell peppers for frozen pepper strips.

Preheat oven to 400°F. Grease 2-quart oblong baking dish. Press rice into bottom of prepared baking dish.

Combine chicken, ⅔ cup French Fried Onions, bell pepper strips, gravy and teriyaki sauce in large bowl; mix well. Pour mixture over rice layer. Cover; bake 30 minutes or until heated through. Top with remaining ⅔ cup onions. Bake 1 minute or until onions are golden.   *Makes 4 to 6 servings*

Prep Time: 10 minutes
Cook Time: 31 minutes

Sausage and Potato Bake

Lightened Up

Spaghetti Pie

4 ounces uncooked thin
   spaghetti
1 egg
¼ cup grated Parmesan cheese
1 teaspoon Italian seasoning
⅔ cup reduced-fat ricotta cheese
½ pound 93% fat-free ground
   turkey
1 teaspoon chili powder
¼ teaspoon crushed fennel seeds
¼ teaspoon ground pepper

⅛ teaspoon ground coriander
1 can (14½ ounces) diced
   tomatoes, undrained
1½ cups sliced fresh mushrooms
1 cup chopped onion
1 can (8 ounces) tomato sauce
¼ cup tomato paste
1 clove garlic, minced
2 teaspoons dried basil leaves
1 cup (4 ounces) shredded part-
   skim mozzarella cheese

1. Cook spaghetti according to package directions, omitting salt. Drain and rinse well under cold water until pasta is cool; drain well.

2. Beat egg, Parmesan cheese and Italian seasoning lightly in medium bowl. Add spaghetti; blend well. Spray deep 9-inch pie plate with nonstick cooking spray. Place spaghetti mixture in pie plate. Press onto bottom and up side of pie plate. Spread ricotta cheese on spaghetti layer.

3. Preheat oven to 350°F. Combine turkey, chili powder, fennel seeds, pepper and coriander in medium bowl. Spray large nonstick skillet with nonstick cooking spray; heat over medium heat until hot. Brown turkey mixture until turkey is no longer pink, stirring to break up meat. Add remaining ingredients except mozzarella cheese. Cook and stir until mixture boils. Spoon mixture over ricotta cheese in pie plate.

4. Cover pie plate with foil. Bake 20 minutes. Remove foil. Sprinkle with mozzarella cheese; bake 5 minutes or until cheese is melted. Let stand before cutting and serving. *Makes 6 servings*

Nutrients per Serving: Calories 294, Total Fat 8 g, Cholesterol 67 mg, Sodium 797 mg

Chicken Casserole Supreme

STUFFING

2 cups unseasoned dry bread crumbs
1 cup chopped green onions
1/3 cup margarine or butter, melted
2 tablespoons chopped fresh parsley

CHICKEN

1/4 cup all-purpose flour
1/4 cup cornmeal
1/4 teaspoon pepper
6 boneless chicken breast halves
    (about 1 1/2 pounds)
1 egg, beaten
1/3 cup margarine or butter

SAUCE

1/4 cup margarine or butter
3 cups sliced fresh mushrooms
1 can (14 1/2 ounces) chicken broth,
    divided
1/3 cup all-purpose flour
3/4 cup HOLLAND HOUSE® Vermouth
    Cooking Wine
1/2 cup whipping cream

In medium bowl, combine all stuffing ingredients; mix well. Place stuffing in 6 mounds in ungreased 13×9-inch baking dish. In shallow dish, combine 1/4 cup flour, cornmeal and pepper. Dip chicken in beaten egg, then coat with flour mixture. Melt 1/3 cup margarine in large skillet. Cook chicken 7 to 8 minutes on each side or until browned. Remove chicken; place on top of stuffing.

Heat oven to 375°F. Melt 1/4 cup margarine in large saucepan. Add mushrooms; cook until tender. Remove from pan. Stir in 1 cup chicken broth and 1/3 cup flour; mix well. Add remaining chicken broth, cooking wine and whipping cream. Cook until slightly thickened, stirring constantly. Stir in mushrooms. Pour over chicken; cover. Bake at 375°F for 1 to 1 1/4 hours or until chicken is tender and no longer pink. *Makes 6 servings*

Chicken-Mac Casserole

1 1/2 cups elbow macaroni, cooked in
    unsalted water and drained
6 slices bacon, fried crisp and
    crumbled
2 cups (10 ounces) cubed cooked
    chicken
1 1/3 cups FRENCH'S® French Fried
    Onions, divided
1 can (10 3/4 ounces) condensed
    cream of mushroom soup
1 cup sour cream
1 package (10 ounces) frozen
    chopped spinach, thawed and
    well drained
1/8 teaspoon garlic powder
1 1/2 cups (6 ounces) shredded Cheddar
    cheese, divided

Preheat oven to 375°F. Return cooked macaroni to saucepan; stir in bacon, chicken and *2/3 cup* French Fried Onions. In medium bowl, combine soup, sour cream, spinach, garlic powder and 1 cup Cheddar cheese. Spoon half the macaroni mixture into greased 12×8-inch baking dish; cover with half the spinach mixture. Repeat layers. Bake, covered, at 375°F for 30 minutes or until heated through. Top with remaining cheese and *2/3 cup* onions. Bake, uncovered, 3 minutes or until onions are golden brown.

Makes 6 to 8 servings

Chicken and Black Bean Enchiladas

2 jars (16 ounces each) mild picante sauce
¼ cup chopped fresh cilantro
2 tablespoons chili powder
1 teaspoon ground cumin
2 cups (10 ounces) chopped cooked chicken
1 can (15 ounces) black beans, drained and rinsed
1⅓ cups FRENCH'S® French Fried Onions, divided
1 package (about 10 ounces) flour tortillas (7 inches)
1 cup (4 ounces) shredded Monterey Jack cheese with jalapeño peppers

Preheat oven 350°F. Grease 10×15-inch jelly-roll baking pan. Combine picante sauce, cilantro, chili powder and cumin in large saucepan. Bring to a boil. Reduce heat to low; simmer 5 minutes.

Combine 1½ cups sauce mixture, chicken, beans and ⅔ *cup* French Fried Onions in medium bowl. Spoon a scant ½ cup filling over bottom third of each tortilla. Roll up tortillas enclosing filling and arrange, seam side down, in a single layer in bottom of prepared baking pan. Spoon remaining sauce evenly over tortillas.

Bake, uncovered, 20 minutes or until heated through. Sprinkle with remaining ⅔ *cup* onions and cheese. Bake 5 minutes or until cheese is melted and onions are golden. Serve immediately.

Makes 5 to 6 servings

Country Wild Rice Casserole

1 cup chopped onion
¼ cup butter or margarine
1¼ pounds ground turkey
¼ teaspoon black pepper
4 cups frozen potatoes O'Brien with onions and peppers, thawed
3 cups cooked wild rice
2 cups shredded mild Cheddar cheese, divided
1 can (10¾ ounces) condensed cream of chicken soup
1 cup sour cream
⅓ cup bread crumbs

Preheat oven to 350°F. In large skillet, sauté onion in butter; remove from skillet. In same skillet, brown turkey. Sprinkle with pepper. Spread potatoes in greased 13×9-inch baking pan. Combine onion, turkey, wild rice, 1½ cups cheese, soup and sour cream in large bowl. Spread onion mixture over potatoes. Sprinkle remaining ½ cup cheese and bread crumbs on top. Bake 40 minutes. *Makes 8 servings*

Favorite recipe from **Minnesota Cultivated Wild Rice Council**

Chicken and Black Bean Enchiladas

Country Classic

Savory Chicken and Biscuits

1 pound boneless, skinless chicken thighs or breasts, cut into 1-inch pieces
1 medium potato, cut into 1-inch pieces
1 medium yellow onion, cut into 1-inch pieces
8 ounces fresh mushrooms, quartered
1 cup fresh baby carrots
1 cup chopped celery
1 (14½-ounce) can chicken broth

3 cloves garlic, minced
1 teaspoon dried rosemary leaves
1 teaspoon salt
1 teaspoon black pepper
3 tablespoons cornstarch blended with ½ cup cold water
1 cup frozen peas, thawed
1 (4-ounce) jar sliced pimentos, drained
1 package BOB EVANS® Frozen Buttermilk Biscuit Dough

Preheat oven to 375°F. Combine chicken, potato, onion, mushrooms, carrots, celery, broth, garlic, rosemary, salt and pepper in large saucepan. Bring to a boil over high heat. Reduce heat to low and simmer, uncovered, 5 minutes. Stir in cornstarch mixture; cook 2 minutes. Stir in peas and pimentos; return to a boil. Transfer chicken mixture to 2-quart casserole dish; arrange frozen biscuits on top. Bake 30 to 35 minutes or until biscuits are golden brown. Refrigerate leftovers. *Makes 4 to 6 servings*

Mediterranean Carrots with Chicken

2 boxes (10 ounces each) BIRDS EYE® frozen Deluxe Baby Whole Carrots
2 cups cubed, cooked chicken breast
3 tablespoons brown sugar
2 tablespoons lemon juice
1 teaspoon cumin

• In large saucepan, combine all ingredients. Cover; cook over medium-low heat 20 minutes or until heated through and carrots are tender.

Makes 4 servings

Prep Time: 5 minutes
Cook Time: 20 minutes

Savory Chicken and Biscuits

Bayou-Style Pot Pie

1 tablespoon olive oil
1 large onion, chopped
1 green bell pepper, chopped
1½ teaspoons bottled minced garlic
8 ounces boneless skinless chicken thighs, cut into 1-inch pieces
1 can (14½ ounces) stewed tomatoes, undrained
8 ounces fully cooked smoked sausage or kielbasa, thinly sliced
¾ teaspoon hot pepper sauce or to taste
2¼ cups buttermilk baking mix
¾ teaspoon dried thyme leaves
⅛ teaspoon black pepper
⅔ cup milk

1. Preheat oven to 450°F. Heat oil in medium ovenproof skillet over medium-high heat until hot. Add onion, bell pepper and garlic. Cook 3 minutes, stirring occasionally.

2. Add chicken and cook 1 minute. Add tomatoes with juice, sausage and hot pepper sauce. Cook, uncovered, over medium-low heat 5 minutes.

3. While chicken is cooking, combine baking mix, thyme and black pepper. Stir in milk. Drop batter by heaping tablespoonfuls in mounds over chicken mixture. Bake 14 minutes or until biscuits are golden brown and cooked through and chicken mixture is bubbly.

Makes 4 servings

Note: You may use any of a variety of fully cooked sausages from your supermarket meat case. Andouille, a fairly spicy Louisiana-style sausage, is perfect for this dish.

Prep and Cook Time: 28 minutes

Turkey á la King

2 cups cubed BUTTERBALL® Fat Free Slice 'N Serve Oven Roasted Breast of Turkey, cubed
⅓ cup butter
4 ounces fresh mushrooms, sliced
4 tablespoons flour
½ teaspoon salt
⅛ teaspoon black pepper
1 can (14½ ounces) chicken broth
½ cup light cream
1 cup frozen peas and carrots
Chopped fresh parsley

Melt butter in large saucepan over medium heat; add mushrooms. Cook and stir 5 minutes. Stir in flour, salt and pepper. Slowly blend in chicken broth and cream. Cook, stirring constantly, until thickened. Add turkey and peas and carrots. Heat well. Serve on toasted thick bread slices or pastry shells, if desired. Sprinkle with chopped parsley.

Makes 4 servings

Prep Time: 25 minutes

Bayou-Style Pot Pie

Creole Chicken Thighs & Rice

    2 tablespoons vegetable oil
2¼ pounds chicken thighs
  ½ teaspoon paprika
  ½ teaspoon dried thyme leaves
  ½ teaspoon salt
  ¼ teaspoon black pepper
  ½ cup chopped celery
  ½ cup chopped green bell pepper
  ½ cup chopped onion
    2 cloves garlic, minced
    1 cup long-grain or converted rice
    1 can (14½ ounces) diced tomatoes,
       undrained
       Hot pepper sauce

Heat oil in large skillet or Dutch oven over medium heat until hot. Add chicken; sprinkle with paprika, thyme, salt and black pepper. Cook 5 to 6 minutes on each side or until golden brown. Remove from skillet.

Add celery, bell pepper, onion and garlic to same skillet; cook 2 minutes. Add rice; cook 2 minutes, stirring to coat rice with oil. Stir in tomatoes with juice, 1 cup water and hot pepper sauce; bring to a boil.

Arrange chicken over rice mixture; reduce heat. Cover; simmer 20 minutes or until chicken is no longer pink in center and liquid is absorbed.

Makes 4 servings

Turkey with Mustard Sauce

1 tablespoon butter or margarine
1 pound turkey cutlets
1 cup BIRDS EYE® frozen Mixed
    Vegetables
1 box (10 ounces) BIRDS EYE® frozen
    Pearl Onions in Cream Sauce
1 teaspoon spicy brown mustard

● In large nonstick skillet, melt butter over medium-high heat. Add turkey; cook until browned on both sides.

● Add mixed vegetables, onions with cream sauce and mustard; bring to boil. Reduce heat to medium-low; cover and simmer 6 to 8 minutes or until vegetables are tender and turkey is no longer pink in center.

Makes 4 servings

Prep Time: 5 minutes
Cook Time: 15 minutes

Creole cooking combines the many flavors of French, Spanish and African cuisines.

Creole Chicken Thighs & Rice

Country Classic

Homestyle Chicken Pot Pie

2 tablespoons margarine or
    butter, divided
1 pound boneless skinless
    chicken breasts, cut into
    1-inch pieces
½ teaspoon salt
½ teaspoon dried thyme leaves
¼ teaspoon black pepper
1 package (16 ounces) frozen
    mixed vegetables, such as
    potatoes, peas and carrots,
    thawed and drained

1 can (10¾ ounces) condensed
    cream of chicken or
    mushroom soup, undiluted
⅓ cup dry white wine or milk
1 refrigerated ready rolled pie
    crust, at room temperature

1. Preheat oven to 425°F. Melt 1 tablespoon margarine in medium broilerproof skillet over medium-high heat. Add chicken; sprinkle with salt, thyme and pepper. Cook 1 minute, stirring frequently.

2. Reduce heat to medium-low. Stir in vegetables, soup and wine; simmer 5 minutes.

3. While soup mixture is simmering, unwrap pie crust. Using a small cookie cutter or apple corer, make 4 decorative cut outs from pastry to allow steam to escape.

4. Remove chicken mixture from heat; top with pie crust. Melt remaining tablespoon margarine. Brush pie crust with 2 teaspoons melted margarine. Arrange cut outs attractively over crust, if desired. Brush cut outs with remaining 1 teaspoon melted margarine. Bake 12 minutes. Turn oven to broil; broil 4 to 5 inches from heat source 2 minutes or until crust is golden brown and chicken mixture is bubbly. *Makes 4 to 5 servings*

Prep and Cook Time: 30 minutes

Homestyle Chicken Pot Pie

Sweet & Sour Cashew Chicken

- 1 can (16 ounces) cling peach slices in syrup
- 1 cup KIKKOMAN® Sweet & Sour Sauce
- 2 boneless, skinless chicken breast halves
- 1 tablespoon cornstarch
- 1 tablespoon KIKKOMAN® Soy Sauce
- 1 tablespoon minced fresh ginger root
- ½ teaspoon sugar
- 2 tablespoons vegetable oil, divided
- 1 onion, chunked
- 1 green bell pepper, chunked
- 1 small carrot, cut diagonally into thin slices
- ⅓ cup roasted cashews

Reserving ⅓ cup syrup, drain peaches; cut slices in half. Blend reserved syrup and sweet & sour sauce; set aside. Cut chicken into 1-inch-square pieces. Combine cornstarch, soy sauce, ginger and sugar in medium bowl; stir in chicken. Heat 1 tablespoon oil in hot wok or large skillet over high heat. Add chicken and stir-fry 4 minutes; remove. Heat remaining 1 tablespoon oil in same pan. Add onion, bell pepper and carrot; stir-fry 4 minutes. Stir in chicken, sweet & sour sauce mixture, peaches and cashews; heat through. Serve immediately. *Makes 4 servings*

Matchstick Stir Fry

- 1 package BUTTERBALL® Fresh Boneless Turkey Breast Strips
- 1 tablespoon cornstarch
- 1 cup orange juice
- 1 tablespoon reduced sodium soy sauce
- 1 clove garlic, minced
- 2 teaspoons grated orange peel
- 2 teaspoons minced fresh ginger
- 1 teaspoon sugar
- ½ teaspoon salt
- ¼ teaspoon red pepper flakes
- 1 tablespoon vegetable oil
- ¼ pound snow peas, trimmed
- 2 small carrots, cut into thin strips
- 1 small onion, cut into strips
- 1 small red bell pepper, cut into thin strips
- 2 oranges, peeled and sectioned

Combine cornstarch, orange juice, soy sauce, garlic, orange peel, ginger, sugar, salt and red pepper flakes in small bowl. Stir until mixture is smooth; set aside. Heat oil in large skillet or wok over high heat until hot; add turkey. Cook and stir 4 to 5 minutes or until turkey is no longer pink; remove from skillet. Add snow peas, carrots, onion and bell pepper. Cook and stir 1 minute; remove from skillet. Add cornstarch mixture to skillet. Cook and stir until mixture thickens; add turkey and vegetables. Reduce heat to low; simmer, covered, 1 minute. Add orange sections. Serve with almond rice, if desired. *Makes 6 servings*

Prep Time: 20 minutes

Sweet & Sour Cashew Chicken

Thai Chicken with Basil

¼ cup vegetable oil
6 large shallots, chopped
5 cloves garlic, minced
1 piece fresh ginger (about 1 inch square), cut into very thin strips
1 pound ground chicken or turkey
2 fresh Thai or jalapeño chilies* (1 red and 1 green or 2 green), seeded and cut into thin slices
2 teaspoons brown sugar
½ teaspoon salt
½ cup thinly sliced basil
Boston lettuce leaves

*Chilies can sting and irritate the skin; wear rubber gloves when handling chilies and do not touch eyes. Wash hands after handling chilies.

Heat oil in wok over medium-high heat 30 seconds or until hot. Add shallots, garlic and ginger; cook and stir 1 minute. Add chicken and stir-fry about 4 minutes or until lightly browned. Push chicken up side of wok, letting juices remain in bottom.

Continue to cook about 5 to 7 minutes until all juices evaporate. Add chili slices, brown sugar and salt to chicken and cook 1 minute. Stir in basil. Remove from heat.

Line serving plate with lettuce. Spoon chicken mixture on top. Garnish as desired. *Makes 4 servings*

Peanut Chicken Stir-Fry

2 tablespoons cornstarch, divided
3 tablespoons KIKKOMAN® Soy Sauce, divided
1 tablespoon dry sherry
1 teaspoon minced garlic, divided
½ pound boneless, skinless chicken breast, cut into thin strips
¼ cup creamy peanut butter
2 teaspoons vinegar
½ teaspoon sugar
⅔ cup water
2 tablespoons vegetable oil, divided
1 bunch green onions and tops, cut into 1-inch lengths
1 red bell pepper, cut into thin strips
¾ pound fresh bean sprouts
Hot cooked fine egg noodles
2 tablespoons chopped unsalted roasted peanuts

Combine 1 tablespoon each cornstarch, soy sauce and sherry with ½ teaspoon garlic in medium bowl; stir in chicken. Let stand 10 minutes. Meanwhile, combine remaining 1 tablespoon cornstarch, 2 tablespoons soy sauce, peanut butter, vinegar and sugar in small bowl; slowly blend in water and set aside. Heat 1 tablespoon oil in hot wok or large skillet over high heat. Add chicken and stir-fry 2 minutes; remove. Heat remaining 1 tablespoon oil in same pan. Add green onions, bell pepper and remaining ½ teaspoon garlic; stir-fry 2 minutes. Add bean sprouts; stir-fry 1 minute longer. Add chicken and peanut butter sauce mixture; cook and stir until sauce boils and thickens. Arrange over noodles and sprinkle peanuts over chicken and vegetables. *Makes 4 servings*

Country Classic

Kung Pao Chicken

1 pound boneless, skinless
   chicken
5 tablespoons KIKKOMAN®
   Stir-Fry Sauce, divided
1 teaspoon vinegar
½ to ¾ teaspoon crushed red
   pepper
¼ teaspoon cornstarch

2 tablespoons water
3 tablespoons vegetable oil,
   divided
1 large clove garlic, minced
1 large onion, chunked
2 small green bell peppers,
   chunked
⅔ cup unsalted roasted peanuts

Cut chicken into 1-inch-square pieces; coat with 1 tablespoon stir-fry sauce in small bowl. Let stand 30 minutes. Meanwhile, combine remaining 4 tablespoons stir-fry sauce, vinegar and crushed red pepper in small bowl; set aside. Dissolve cornstarch in water in small bowl; set aside. Heat 1 tablespoon oil in hot wok or large skillet over high heat. Add chicken and garlic and stir-fry 3 minutes; remove. Heat remaining 2 tablespoons oil in same pan. Add onion; stir-fry 1 minute. Add bell peppers; stir-fry 4 minutes longer. Add chicken, stir-fry sauce mixture, cornstarch mixture and peanuts; cook and stir until sauce boils and thickens. *Makes 4 servings*

Stir-Fry Empress Lemon Chicken

2 tablespoons cornstarch
4 tablespoons KIKKOMAN® Soy
   Sauce, divided
1 pound boneless, skinless chicken,
   cut into 1-inch pieces
½ cup sugar
2½ teaspoons cornstarch
¾ teaspoon grated lemon peel
2 tablespoons lemon juice
2 tablespoons vegetable oil
1 bunch green onions, cut into
   1-inch lengths

Combine 2 tablespoons cornstarch and 1 tablespoon soy sauce; stir in chicken. Let stand 30 minutes. Meanwhile, combine sugar, ¼ cup water, remaining 3 tablespoons soy sauce, 2½ teaspoons cornstarch, lemon peel and juice; set aside. Heat oil in hot wok over high heat. Add chicken and green onions; stir-fry 3 minutes. Remove. Reduce heat to medium-high. Pour soy sauce mixture into wok; bring to boil. Cook, stirring constantly, 1 minute. Add chicken and green onions, stirring to coat all pieces well with sauce. Serve immediately. *Makes 4 servings*

Ginger Chicken Stir-Fry

1 whole chicken breast, skinned and boned
4 tablespoons KIKKOMAN® Teriyaki Marinade & Sauce, divided
3 teaspoons minced fresh ginger root, divided
1 cup water
2 tablespoons cornstarch
2 tablespoons vegetable oil, divided
2 carrots, cut into julienne strips
1 medium onion, sliced
¾ pound fresh spinach, washed, drained and torn in half

Cut chicken into thin strips. Combine 1 tablespoon teriyaki sauce and 2 teaspoons ginger in small bowl; stir in chicken. Let stand 10 minutes. Meanwhile, combine water, remaining 3 tablespoons teriyaki sauce, 1 teaspoon ginger and cornstarch in small bowl; set aside. Heat 1 tablespoon oil in hot wok or large skillet over high heat. Add chicken and stir-fry 2 minutes; remove. Heat remaining 1 tablespoon oil in same pan. Add carrots and onion; stir-fry 2 minutes. Add chicken and teriyaki sauce mixture; cook and stir until sauce boils and thickens. Stir in spinach; serve immediately. *Makes 4 servings*

Sweet and Spicy Chicken Stir-Fry

1½ cups uncooked long-grain white rice
1 can (8 ounces) DEL MONTE® FreshCut™ Brand Pineapple Chunks In Its Own Juice, undrained
4 boneless, skinless chicken breast halves, cut into bite-size pieces
2 tablespoons vegetable oil
1 large green bell pepper, cut into strips
¾ cup sweet and sour sauce
⅛ to ½ teaspoon red pepper flakes

1. Cook rice according to package directions.

2. Drain pineapple, reserving ⅓ cup juice.

3. Stir-fry chicken in hot oil in large skillet over medium-high heat until no longer pink in center. Add green pepper and reserved pineapple juice; stir-fry 2 minutes or until tender-crisp.

4. Add sweet and sour sauce, red pepper flakes and pineapple; stir-fry 3 minutes or until heated through.

5. Spoon rice onto serving plate; top with chicken mixture. Garnish, if desired. *Makes 4 servings*

Prep Time: 5 minutes
Cook Time: 20 minutes

Ginger Chicken Stir-Fry

Lightened Up

Sweet and Sour Stir-Fry

1 tablespoon vegetable oil
1 pound boneless skinless
    chicken breasts, cut into
    3-inch strips
1 can (8 ounces) sliced water
    chestnuts, drained
1 cup 2×1/2-inch red bell pepper
    strips
1/4 cup chopped onion
2 tablespoons cornstarch
2 tablespoons soy sauce
1 tablespoon white vinegar

1 can (8 ounces) pineapple
    chunks, packed in juice,
    undrained
1/4 teaspoon ground ginger
1/4 teaspoon salt
1 3/4 teaspoons EQUAL® Measure™
    or 6 packets EQUAL®
    sweetener or 1/4 cup EQUAL®
    Spoonful™
1 package (6 ounces) frozen pea
    pods

● Heat oil in wok or skillet. Add chicken; cook until chicken is no longer pink, 5 to 6 minutes. Remove and set aside. Add water chestnuts, pepper and onion to wok; cook until vegetables are tender, 3 to 4 minutes, stirring constantly.

● Combine cornstarch, soy sauce and vinegar in small bowl; stir to dissolve cornstarch. Add pineapple with juice, ginger and salt. Add to vegetable mixture; cook until sauce thickens, 2 to 3 minutes, stirring constantly.

● Stir in EQUAL®. Add pea pods and chicken; cook until pea pods and chicken are heated through, 2 to 3 minutes.   *Makes 4 servings*

Nutrients per Serving: Calories 272, Total Fat 5 g, Cholesterol 66 mg, Sodium 620 mg

First Moon Chicken Stir-Fry

2 tablespoons cornstarch, divided
3 tablespoons KIKKOMAN® Soy Sauce, divided
2½ teaspoons sugar, divided
1 clove garlic, pressed
2 boneless, skinless chicken breast halves, cut into 1-inch squares
¾ cup water
1 teaspoon distilled white vinegar
½ pound fresh broccoli, trimmed
2 tablespoons vegetable oil, divided
1 medium onion, chunked
1 small carrot, cut diagonally into thin slices
½ teaspoon crushed red pepper
¼ pound fresh snow peas, trimmed and cut diagonally into halves

Combine 1 tablespoon each cornstarch and soy sauce with ½ teaspoon sugar and garlic in medium bowl; stir in chicken. Let stand 15 minutes. Meanwhile, combine water, remaining 2 tablespoons soy sauce, 1 tablespoon cornstarch, 2 teaspoons sugar and vinegar in small bowl; set aside. Remove flowerets from broccoli; cut into bite-size pieces. Peel stalks; cut diagonally into thin slices. Heat 1 tablespoon oil in hot wok or large skillet over high heat. Add chicken and stir-fry 3 minutes; remove. Heat remaining 1 tablespoon oil in same pan. Add broccoli, onion, carrot and crushed red pepper; stir-fry 3 minutes. Add snow peas; stir-fry 2 minutes longer. Add chicken and soy sauce mixture; cook and stir until sauce boils and thickens. *Makes 4 servings*

Chicken Stir-Fry

4 boneless, skinless chicken breast halves (about 1½ pounds)
2 tablespoons vegetable oil
1 tablespoon cornstarch
2 tablespoons light soy sauce
2 tablespoons orange juice
1 bag (16 ounces) BIRDS EYE® frozen Farm Fresh Mixtures Broccoli, Carrots & Water Chestnuts

●Cut chicken into ½-inch-thick long strips.

●In wok or large skillet, heat oil over medium-high heat.

●Add chicken; cook 5 minutes, stirring occasionally.

●Meanwhile, in small bowl, combine cornstarch, soy sauce and orange juice; blend well and set aside.

●Add vegetables to chicken; cook 5 minutes more or until chicken is no longer pink in center, stirring occasionally.

●Stir in soy sauce mixture; cook 1 minute or until heated through.
Makes 4 servings

Serving Suggestion: Serve over hot cooked rice.

Prep Time: 5 minutes
Cook Time: 12 minutes

First Moon Chicken Stir-Fry

Chicken Soup au Pistou

Olive oil-flavored nonstick cooking spray
½ pound boneless, skinless chicken breasts, cut into ½-inch pieces
1 large onion, diced
3 cans (14½ ounces each) chicken broth
1 can (15 ounces) whole tomatoes, undrained
1 can (14 ounces) great Northern beans, rinsed and drained
2 medium carrots, sliced
1 large potato, diced
¼ teaspoon salt
¼ teaspoon black pepper
1 cup frozen Italian green beans
¼ cup prepared pesto
Grated Parmesan cheese (optional)

Spray large saucepan with cooking spray; heat over medium-high heat until hot. Add chicken; cook and stir about 5 minutes or until chicken is browned. Add onion; cook and stir 2 minutes.

Add chicken broth, tomatoes with juice, great Northern beans, carrots, potato, salt and pepper. Bring to a boil, stirring to break up tomatoes. Reduce heat to low. Cover and simmer 15 minutes, stirring occasionally. Add green beans; cook about 5 minutes more or until vegetables are tender.

Ladle soup into bowls. Top with teaspoonful pesto and sprinkle with Parmesan cheese, if desired.

Makes about 8 (1½-cup) servings

Garden Patch Turkey Stew with Dumplings

3 cups cubed cooked BUTTERBALL® Turkey (1 pound)
1 medium onion, sliced
2 ribs celery, sliced
2 tablespoons butter or margarine
2 cups coarsely chopped cabbage
1 can (14½ ounces) tomatoes, undrained, cut up
1 can (15 ounces) kidney beans, undrained
2 cans (13¾ ounces each) chicken broth
1 cup water
2 tablespoons sugar
1½ teaspoons dried marjoram leaves, crushed
1 teaspoon salt
2 cups buttermilk baking mix
⅔ cup milk

Cook and stir onion and celery in butter in Dutch oven or large saucepan over medium heat until crisp-tender. Add turkey, cabbage, tomatoes, beans, broth, water, sugar, marjoram and salt. Cover; reduce heat to low and simmer 25 minutes or until cabbage is tender. Place baking mix in medium bowl. Stir in milk with fork until soft dough forms. Bring stew to a boil over high heat. Drop dough by spoonfuls into boiling stew to make 12 dumplings. Reduce heat to low. Cover and simmer 15 minutes. Serve in bowls.

Makes 6 to 8 servings (12 cups)

Chicken Soup au Pistou

Bandstand Chili

    2 cups chopped cooked
        BUTTERBALL® Boneless Young
        Turkey
    1 tablespoon vegetable oil
 1½ cups chopped onions
 1½ cups chopped red bell pepper
    2 tablespoons mild Mexican
        seasoning*
    1 clove garlic, minced
    1 can (28 ounces) tomato purée with
        tomato bits
    1 can (15½ ounces) light red kidney
        beans, undrained

*To make your own Mexican seasoning,
combine 1 tablespoon chili powder, 1½
teaspoons oregano and 1½ teaspoons cumin.

Heat oil in large skillet over medium
heat until hot. Add onions, bell pepper,
Mexican seasoning and garlic. Cook
and stir 4 to 5 minutes. Add tomato
purée and beans; stir in turkey. Reduce
heat to low; simmer 5 minutes.

Makes 8 servings

Sweet potatoes are rich

in vitamins A and C.

Their high sugar

content is responsible

for their sweetness.

Home-Style Chicken and Sweet Potato Stew

    4 boneless, skinless chicken breasts
        Garlic salt and pepper
    ½ cup all-purpose flour
    ¼ cup WESSON® Vegetable Oil
    2 cups cubed, peeled sweet potatoes
    1 cup chopped onion
    1 (14.5-ounce) can HUNT'S® Stewed
        Tomatoes, lightly crushed
    ¾ cup homemade chicken stock or
        canned chicken broth
    ¾ cup apple cider
    ½ teaspoon dried dill weed
    1 chicken bouillon cube
        Dash or two of GEBHARDT® Hot
        Pepper Sauce
        Salt to taste

Rinse chicken and pat dry; cut into
½-inch pieces. Sprinkle with garlic salt
and pepper. Place flour in plastic bag.
Add chicken; shake until chicken is
well coated. In large stockpot, heat
Wesson Oil. Add chicken; cook on both
sides until golden brown. Remove
chicken; set aside. In same pot, add
sweet potatoes and onion; sauté until
onion is tender. Stir in remaining
ingredients except salt; blend well. Add
browned chicken; bring to a boil.
Reduce heat; cover and simmer 25 to
30 minutes or until chicken is no longer
pink in center and potatoes are tender,
stirring often. Salt to taste.

Makes 4 servings

Pure Wesson®: For a sweeter stew,
substitute yams for sweet potatoes.

Bandstand Chili

Country Classic

Creamy Wild Rice and Turkey Soup

2 cups chopped cooked BUTTERBALL® Breast of Young Turkey	2 cloves garlic, minced
1 tablespoon olive oil	2 cans (14½ ounces each) chicken broth
1 cup finely chopped carrots	2 cups cooked wild rice
1 cup finely chopped onion	½ cup whipping cream
½ cup finely chopped celery	Salt and black pepper

Heat oil in large saucepan over medium heat until hot. Cook and stir carrots, onion, celery and garlic until onion is soft. Add chicken broth, wild rice and turkey; heat 10 minutes. Add whipping cream; cook over low heat until heated through. Add salt and pepper to taste. *Makes 8 (1-cup) servings*

Prep Time: 30 minutes

White Chili

1 pound ground turkey
2 cloves garlic, finely chopped
2 cans (15 ounces each) white kidney beans, undrained
2 cans (4 ounces each) chopped green chilies, undrained
1⅓ cups FRENCH'S® French Fried Onions, divided
1 cup frozen whole kernel corn
¼ cup chopped fresh cilantro
3 tablespoons lime juice
1 tablespoon ground cumin
¼ teaspoon ground white pepper
1 large tomato, chopped
¼ cup low-fat sour cream

Heat large nonstick skillet or Dutch oven over medium heat. Add turkey and garlic; cook and stir about 5 minutes or until turkey is no longer pink.

Stir in beans, green chilies, ⅔ cup French Fried Onions, corn, cilantro, lime juice, cumin and white pepper. Bring to a boil over high heat. Reduce heat to low; simmer 5 minutes, stirring often.

Stir in tomato and sour cream; cook until hot and bubbly, stirring often. Sprinkle with remaining ⅔ cup onions.
Makes 4 to 6 servings

Prep Time: 15 minutes
Cook Time: 20 minutes

Chicken Stew with Dumplings

2 tablespoons vegetable oil
2 cups sliced carrots
1 cup chopped onion
1 large green pepper, sliced
½ cup sliced celery
2 cans (14½ ounces each) fat-free reduced-sodium chicken broth
¼ cup plus 2 tablespoons all-purpose flour
2 pounds boneless, skinless chicken breasts, cut into 1-inch pieces
3 medium potatoes, unpeeled and cut into 1-inch pieces
6 ounces mushrooms, halved
¾ cup frozen peas
1 teaspoon dried basil
¾ teaspoon dried rosemary
¼ teaspoon dried tarragon
¾ to 1 teaspoon salt
¼ teaspoon black pepper

HERB DUMPLINGS

2 cups biscuit mix
½ teaspoon dried basil
½ teaspoon dried rosemary
¼ teaspoon dried tarragon
⅔ cup reduced-fat (2%) milk

1. Heat oil in Dutch oven until hot. Add carrots, onion, green pepper and celery; cook and stir until onion is tender. Stir in broth, reserving ½ cup; bring to a boil. Mix reserved ½ cup broth and flour; stir into boiling mixture. Boil, stirring constantly, 1 minute or until thickened. Stir chicken, potatoes, mushrooms, peas and herbs into mixture. Reduce heat to low; simmer, covered, 18 to 20 minutes or until chicken is no longer pink in center. Add salt and pepper.

2. For Herb Dumplings, combine biscuit mix and herbs in small bowl; stir in milk to form soft dough. Spoon dumpling mixture on top of stew in 8 large spoonfuls. Reduce heat to low. Cook, uncovered, 10 minutes. Cover and cook 10 minutes or until biscuits are tender and toothpick inserted in center comes out clean. Serve in shallow bowls.

Makes 8 (1¼-cup) servings

Turkey Tortilla Soup

1 package (1¼ pounds) BUTTERBALL® Lean Fresh Ground Turkey
1 teaspoon olive oil
2 cans (14½ ounces each) 100% fat free reduced sodium chicken broth
1 jar (16 ounces) mild or medium-hot salsa
1 can (11 ounces) Mexican-style corn, drained
1 tablespoon fresh lime juice
2 to 3 tablespoons chopped fresh cilantro
Salt and black pepper
2 ounces baked tortilla chips
Lime wedges

Heat oil in large saucepan over medium heat until hot. Brown turkey in saucepan 6 to 8 minutes or until no longer pink, stirring to separate meat. Add chicken broth, salsa, corn and lime juice to saucepan. Reduce heat to low; simmer, covered, about 10 minutes. Ladle into bowls. Sprinkle with cilantro. Add salt and pepper to taste. Serve with tortilla chips and wedge of lime.

Makes 8 servings

Country Chicken Chowder

1 pound chicken tenders
2 tablespoons margarine or butter
1 small onion, chopped
1 rib celery, sliced
1 small carrot, sliced
1 can (10¾ ounces) cream of potato soup
1 cup milk
1 cup frozen corn
½ teaspoon dried dill weed

Cut chicken tenders into ½-inch pieces. Melt margarine in large saucepan over medium-high heat. Add chicken; cook and stir 5 minutes. Add onion, celery and carrot; cook and stir 3 minutes. Stir in soup, milk, corn and dill; reduce heat to low. Cook about 8 minutes or until corn is tender and chowder is heated through. Add salt and pepper to taste.

Makes 4 servings

Quick-cooking barley cooks in one third of the time of regular barley. It's readily available in supermarkets.

Hearty Turkey Soup

8 ounces BUTTERBALL® Fat Free Turkey Smoked Sausage, cut into chunks
8 ounces fresh mushrooms, quartered
½ large onion, chunked
2 medium carrots, sliced
3 large cloves garlic, minced
3 medium red potatoes, cubed
1 can (14½ ounces) diced tomatoes with roasted garlic
1 can (14½ ounces) low salt, 98% fat free chicken broth
¼ cup quick-cook barley
1 can (15 ounces) small white beans
¼ cup chopped fresh Italian parsley
Salt and black pepper
Grated Parmesan cheese

Spray large heavy saucepan with nonstick cooking spray. Add mushrooms, onion, carrots and garlic; cook over medium heat, stirring constantly, about 5 minutes. Add potatoes, tomatoes, chicken broth and barley. Cover; simmer about 10 minutes. Stir in undrained beans, sausage and parsley. Simmer 5 minutes. Add salt and pepper to taste. Serve with grated Parmesan cheese.

Makes 8 servings

Prep Time: 30 to 40 minutes

Country Chicken Chowder

Fish Creole

1 pound fresh or thawed frozen snapper or sole fillets
1 bag (16 ounces) BIRDS EYE® frozen Farm Fresh Mixtures Broccoli, Green Beans, Pearl Onions & Red Peppers
1 can (16 ounces) tomato sauce
1 tablespoon dried oregano or Italian seasoning
1 tablespoon vegetable oil
1½ teaspoons salt

- Preheat oven to 350°F.
- Place fish in 13×9-inch baking pan.
- In large bowl, combine vegetables, tomato sauce, oregano, oil and salt.
- Pour vegetable mixture over fish.
- Bake 20 minutes or until fish flakes easily when tested with fork.

Makes 4 servings

Prep Time: 5 minutes
Cook Time: 20 minutes

Fish Creole

Lightened Up

Impossibly Easy Salmon Pie

1 can (7½ ounces) salmon packed in water, drained, deboned
½ cup grated Parmesan cheese
¼ cup sliced green onions
1 jar (2 ounces) chopped pimiento, drained
½ cup low-fat (1%) cottage cheese
1 tablespoon lemon juice

1½ cups low-fat (1%) milk
¾ cup reduced-fat baking and pancake mix
2 whole eggs
2 egg whites *or* ¼ cup cholesterol-free egg substitute
¼ teaspoon dried dill weed
¼ teaspoon salt
¼ teaspoon paprika (optional)

1. Preheat oven to 375°F. Spray 9-inch pie plate with nonstick cooking spray. Combine salmon, Parmesan cheese, onions and pimiento in prepared pie plate; set aside.

2. Combine cottage cheese and lemon juice in blender or food processor; purée until smooth. Add milk, baking mix, whole eggs, egg whites, dill and salt. Blend 15 seconds. Pour over salmon mixture. Sprinkle with paprika, if desired.

3. Bake 35 to 40 minutes or until lightly golden and knife inserted halfway between center and edge comes out clean. Cool 5 minutes before serving. Garnish as desired.
Makes 8 servings

Nutrients per Serving: Calories 192, Total Fat 6 g, Cholesterol 75 mg, Sodium 656 mg

Impossibly Easy Salmon Pie

By-the-Sea Casserole

1 bag (16 ounces) BIRDS EYE® frozen
    Mixed Vegetables
2 cans (6½ ounces each) tuna in
    water, drained
1 cup uncooked instant rice
1 can (10¾ ounces) cream of celery
    soup
1 cup 1% milk
1 cup cheese-flavored fish-shaped
    crackers

• **Microwave Directions:** In medium
bowl, combine vegetables and tuna.

• Stir in rice, soup and milk.

• Place tuna mixture in 1½-quart
microwave-safe casserole dish; cover
and microwave on HIGH 6 minutes.
Stir; microwave, covered, 6 to 8
minutes more or until rice is tender.

• Stir casserole and sprinkle with
crackers. *Makes 6 servings*

Prep Time: 10 minutes
Cook Time: 15 minutes

*Feta is a classic
Greek cheese that has a
salty, tangy flavor.*

Mediterranean Catch

2 medium onions, sliced
1 small green and red bell peppers,
    cut into thin strips
2 tablespoons olive oil
2 large tomatoes, cut into thin
    wedges
3 cloves garlic, minced
2 pounds firm-textured fish fillets
    (such as codfish, grouper or red
    snapper)
1 (8-ounce) package ATHENOS® Feta
    Natural Cheese, crumbled
1 tablespoon chopped fresh parsley

• Heat oven to 375°F.

• Cook and stir onions and peppers in
oil in large skillet over medium-high
heat 5 minutes or until tender-crisp.
Add tomatoes and garlic; mix lightly.

• Arrange fish in single layer in 13×9-
inch baking dish. Spoon vegetable
mixture over fish; sprinkle with cheese.

• Bake 25 minutes or until fish flakes
easily with fork. Sprinkle with parsley.
Season to taste with salt and pepper.
Makes 4 to 6 servings

Variation: Substitute 1 (8-ounce)
package ATHENOS® Feta Natural
Cheese with Peppercorn for regular Feta
Cheese.

By-the-Sea Casserole

Tuna Quesadilla Stack

4 (10-inch) flour tortillas, divided
¼ cup plus 2 tablespoons pinto or black bean dip
1 can (9 ounces) tuna packed in water, drained and flaked
2 cups (8 ounces) shredded Cheddar cheese
1 can (14½ ounces) diced tomatoes, drained
½ cup thinly sliced green onions
½ tablespoon butter or margarine, melted

1. Preheat oven to 400°F.

2. Place 1 tortilla on 12-inch pizza pan. Spread with 2 tablespoons bean dip, leaving ½-inch border. Top with one third each of tuna, cheese, tomatoes and green onions. Repeat layers twice beginning with tortilla and ending with onions.

3. Top with remaining tortilla, pressing gently. Brush with melted butter.

4. Bake 15 minutes or until cheese melts and top is lightly browned. Cool and cut into 8 wedges.

Makes 4 servings

Tip: For a special touch, serve with assorted toppings, such as prepared avocado dip, sour cream and salsa.

Prep and Cook Time: 25 minutes

Herbed Fish Roll-Ups

1 cup cooked wild rice
1 cup shredded zucchini
2 tablespoons chopped fresh parsley
1 teaspoon Dijon mustard
1 teaspoon lemon juice
1 teaspoon Worcestershire sauce
½ teaspoon garlic powder
¼ teaspoon pepper
¼ teaspoon dried tarragon leaves
¼ teaspoon dried thyme leaves
8 (4- to 5-ounce) white fish fillets, such as sole or haddock
8 HEALTHY CHOICE® Fat Free Natural Mozzarella Cheese Snack Stix
Paprika

Heat oven to 375°F. For filling, combine all ingredients except fish, cheese and paprika. Place about 2 tablespoons of filling in center of each fish fillet; top with cheese stick. Roll up and place seam side down in 12×7-inch baking dish sprayed with nonstick cooking spray. Bake at 375°F for 20 to 25 minutes until fish flakes with a fork and cheese is melted. Sprinkle fish with paprika before serving.

Makes 8 servings

Tuna Quesadilla Stack

Country Classic

Quick Cajun Jambalaya

3 tablespoons butter
1 onion, diced
1 *each* red and green bell
    pepper, diced
12 slices HILLSHIRE FARM® Ham,
    cut into ½-inch strips
12 large raw shrimp, peeled and
    deveined
1 can (28 ounces) crushed
    tomatoes, undrained

2 teaspoons salt
¼ teaspoon garlic powder
¼ teaspoon red pepper flakes
¼ teaspoon black pepper
¼ teaspoon hot pepper sauce
6 cups cooked white rice
    Cajun Garlic Bread (recipe
    follows)

Heat butter in large saucepan over medium-high heat; cook onion and bell peppers until soft, about 5 minutes. Add Ham and shrimp; cook until shrimp turn pink, about 3 minutes. Add tomatoes with liquid, seasonings and rice; cook 5 minutes or until heated through. Serve with Cajun Garlic Bread.

Makes 6 servings

Cajun Garlic Bread

¼ teaspoon garlic powder
⅛ teaspoon ground red pepper
⅛ teaspoon dried oregano or
    basil leaves

2 tablespoons butter, melted
1 loaf French bread, cut
    lengthwise into halves

Preheat oven to 350°F. Stir garlic powder, pepper and oregano into butter in small bowl. Drizzle butter mixture over cut sides of bread. Reassemble loaf; wrap in foil. Bake 10 minutes.

Makes 6 servings

Quick Cajun Jambalaya

Thai-Style Tuna Fried Rice

> 4 to 5 tablespoons vegetable oil, divided
> 2 eggs, lightly beaten
> $2/3$ cup uncooked, peeled medium shrimp, chopped into $3/4$-inch pieces
> 3 cloves garlic
> 1 to 2 tablespoons minced fresh serrano chiles
> 4 to 6 cups cooked rice, chilled overnight
> 1 tablespoon sugar
> 1 tablespoon nam pla (fish sauce) (optional)
> 1 tablespoon soy sauce
> 1 can (6 ounces) STARKIST® Solid White or Chunk Light Tuna, drained and chunked
> $1/2$ cup chopped dry-roasted peanuts
> $1/4$ cup chopped fresh basil
> 2 tablespoons chopped fresh cilantro
> Lime wedges for garnish

In wok, heat 1 tablespoon oil over medium-high heat; add eggs and cook, stirring, until partially cooked but still runny. Return eggs to bowl. Wipe out wok with paper towels. Add 2 tablespoons oil to wok; heat.

Add shrimp, garlic and chiles. Stir-fry until shrimp turn pink, about 3 minutes. Remove shrimp mixture; set aside. Add 1 or 2 tablespoons oil to wok; stir-fry rice, sugar, nam pla, if desired, and soy sauce until rice is heated through. Add tuna and peanuts; heat.

Return shrimp mixture and eggs to pan, chopping eggs into pieces with stir-fry spatula. Add basil and cilantro; toss

gently to mix. Serve with lime wedges for garnish; squeeze juice on fried rice, if desired. *Makes 4 to 6 servings*

Prep and Cook Time: 15 minutes

Mediterranean Cod

> 1 bag (16 ounces) BIRDS EYE® frozen Farm Fresh Mixtures Broccoli, Green Beans, Pearl Onions and Red Peppers
> 1 can ($14^{1/2}$ ounces) stewed tomatoes
> $1/2$ teaspoon dried basil leaves
> 1 pound cod fillets, cut into serving pieces
> $1/2$ cup orange juice
> 2 tablespoons all-purpose flour
> $1/4$ cup sliced black olives (optional)

● Combine vegetables, tomatoes and basil in large skillet. Bring to boil over medium-high heat.

● Place cod on vegetables. Pour $1/4$ cup orange juice over fish. Cover and cook 5 to 7 minutes or until fish is tender and flakes with fork.

● Remove cod and keep warm. Blend flour with remaining $1/4$ cup orange juice; stir into skillet. Cook until liquid is thickened and vegetables are coated.

● Serve fish with vegetables; sprinkle with olives. *Makes about 4 servings*

Serving Suggestion: Serve with rice or couscous.

Prep Time: 5 minutes
Cook Time: 15 minutes

Lightened Up

Shrimp in Tomatillo Sauce over Rice

1 teaspoon olive oil
¼ cup chopped onion
1 cup GUILTLESS GOURMET®
    Green Tomatillo Salsa
¾ cup white wine

Juice of ½ lemon
12 ounces medium-size raw
    shrimp, peeled and deveined
4 cups hot cooked white rice
Lemon peel strip (optional)

Heat oil in large nonstick skillet over medium-high heat until hot. Add onion; cook and stir until onion is translucent. Add salsa, wine and juice, stirring just until mixture begins to boil. Reduce heat to medium-low; simmer 10 minutes. Add shrimp; cook about 2 minutes or until shrimp turn pink and opaque, stirring occasionally. To serve, place 1 cup rice in each of 4 individual serving bowls. Pour shrimp mixture evenly over rice. Garnish with lemon peel, if desired.

Makes 4 servings

Nutrients per Serving: Calories 274, Total Fat 2 g, Cholesterol 130 mg, Sodium 479 mg

Jazzy Jambalaya

1 package (6.8 ounces) RICE-A-
    RONI® Spanish Rice
1 cup chopped cooked chicken or
    ham
1 cup chopped onion
1 cup chopped green bell pepper
2 cloves garlic, minced
3 tablespoons vegetable oil
1 can (14½ ounces) tomatoes,
    undrained and chopped
Dash hot pepper sauce (optional)
½ pound raw shrimp, shelled,
    deveined *or* 8 ounces frozen
    cleaned precooked shrimp

1. In large skillet, combine rice-vermicelli mix, chicken, onion, green pepper, garlic and oil. Sauté over medium heat, stirring frequently, until vermicelli is golden brown.

2. Stir in 2 cups water, tomatoes, hot pepper sauce and contents of seasoning packet; bring to a boil over high heat.

3. Cover; reduce heat. Simmer 10 minutes.

4. Stir in shrimp.

5. Cover; continue cooking 8 to 10 minutes or until liquid is absorbed, rice is tender and shrimp turn pink.

Makes 5 servings

Shrimp Primavera Pot Pie

1 can (10¾ ounces) condensed
    cream of shrimp soup, undiluted
1 package (12 ounces) frozen peeled
    uncooked medium shrimp
2 packages (1 pound each) frozen
    mixed vegetables, such as green
    beans, potatoes, onions and red
    peppers, thawed and drained
1 teaspoon dried dill weed
¼ teaspoon salt
¼ teaspoon black pepper
1 package (11 ounces) refrigerated
    soft breadstick dough

1. Preheat oven to 400°F. Heat soup in medium ovenproof skillet over medium-high heat 1 minute. Add shrimp; cook and stir 3 minutes or until shrimp begin to thaw. Stir in vegetables, dill, salt and pepper; mix well. Reduce heat to medium-low; cook and stir 3 minutes.

2. Unwrap breadstick dough; separate into 8 strips. Twist strips, cutting to fit skillet. Arrange attractively over shrimp mixture. Press ends of dough lightly to edges of skillet to secure. Bake 18 minutes or until crust is golden brown and shrimp mixture is bubbly.

Makes 4 to 6 servings

Prep and Cook Time: 30 minutes

Shrimp Classico

⅔ cup milk
2 tablespoons margarine or butter
1 package (4.8 ounces) PASTA RONI®
    Angel Hair Pasta with Herbs
1 clove garlic, minced
1 package (10 ounces) frozen
    chopped spinach, thawed and
    well drained
1 package (10 ounces) frozen
    precooked shrimp, thawed and
    well drained
1 jar (2 ounces) chopped pimentos,
    drained

1. **Microwave Directions**: In 3-quart round microwavable glass casserole, combine 1⅔ cups water, milk and margarine. Microwave, uncovered, at HIGH 4 to 5 minutes or until boiling.

2. Gradually add pasta while stirring. Separate pasta with a fork, if needed. Stir in contents of seasoning packet and garlic.

3. Microwave, uncovered, at HIGH 4 minutes, stirring gently after 2 minutes. Separate pasta with a fork, if needed. Stir in spinach, shrimp and pimentos. Microwave at HIGH 1 to 2 minutes. Sauce will be very thin, but will thicken upon standing.

4. Let stand, uncovered, 2 minutes or until desired consistency. Stir before serving. *Makes 4 servings*

Shrimp Primavera Pot Pie

Seafood Risotto

1 package (5.2 ounces) rice in
  creamy sauce (Risotto Milanese
  flavor)
1 package (14 to 16 ounces) frozen
  fully cooked shrimp
1 box (10 ounces) BIRDS EYE® frozen
  Mixed Vegetables
2 teaspoons grated Parmesan cheese

• In 4-quart saucepan, prepare rice
according to package directions. Add
frozen shrimp and vegetables during
last 10 minutes.

• Sprinkle with cheese.

Makes 4 servings

Serving Suggestion: Serve with garlic
bread and a tossed green salad.

Prep Time: 5 minutes
Cook Time: 15 minutes

*Risotto is a creamy
Italian rice dish made
with arborio rice.*

Crab and Scallop Creole

1 tablespoon vegetable oil
1 large onion, chopped
1 large green bell pepper, chopped
2 cloves garlic, minced
1 can (15 ounces) crushed tomatoes,
  undrained
3 to 4 tablespoons FRANK'S®
  Original REDHOT® Cayenne
  Pepper Sauce, divided
½ teaspoon dried basil leaves
½ teaspoon dried thyme leaves
1 package (9 ounces) frozen corn
½ pound raw bay scallops
½ pound crabmeat or imitation
  crabmeat, flaked (2 cups)
Cooked white rice (optional)

1. Heat oil in large nonstick skillet over
medium-high heat. Add onion, bell
pepper and garlic; cook until tender.
Add tomatoes with liquid, 2 to 3
tablespoons RedHot® sauce, basil and
thyme. Cover; cook over medium-low
heat 10 minutes, stirring occasionally.

2. Add corn and scallops. Bring to a
boil. Reduce heat to low. Cover; cook
5 minutes or until scallops are
translucent. Stir in crabmeat; heat
through.

3. Stir in 1 to 2 tablespoons RedHot®
sauce. Serve over rice, if desired.

Makes 4 servings

Prep Time: 20 minutes
Cook Time: 20 minutes

Seafood Risotto

Scallops & Snow Peas

¾ **pound fresh or thawed bay scallops**
¾ **cup water**
2 **tablespoons KIKKOMAN® Soy Sauce**
2 **tablespoons dry white wine**
4 **teaspoons cornstarch**
½ **teaspoon sugar**
3 **small dried whole red chili peppers**
1 **tablespoon vegetable oil**
1 **medium onion, cut into 1-inch pieces**
2 **teaspoons slivered fresh ginger root**
½ **pound fresh snow peas, trimmed and cut diagonally into halves**
1½ **teaspoons Oriental sesame oil**

Cook scallops in small amount of boiling water 30 seconds; drain. Combine ¾ cup water, soy sauce, wine, cornstarch and sugar in small bowl; set aside. Cut each chili pepper open lengthwise, being careful not to cut all the way through; set aside. Heat vegetable oil in hot wok or large skillet over medium heat; add chilies and stir-fry 30 seconds. Remove chilies; increase heat to high. Add onion and ginger; stir-fry 1 minute. Add snow peas; stir-fry 2 minutes longer. Add scallops, chilies and soy sauce mixture; cook and stir until sauce boils and thickens. Remove from heat and stir in sesame oil. Serve immediately.

Makes 4 servings

Shrimp with Strawberries and Snow Peas

1 **tablespoon vegetable oil**
½ **pound peeled medium shrimp**
¼ **pound snow peas**
2 **ounces fresh bean sprouts, rinsed**
2 **cloves garlic, minced**
½ **teaspoon minced fresh ginger**
2 **tablespoons brown sugar**
2 **tablespoons soy sauce**
1 **tablespoon dark sesame oil**
2 **teaspoons balsamic vinegar**
2 **teaspoons oyster sauce**
1 **cup strawberries, washed, hulled and quartered**
2 **cups hot cooked rice**

1. Heat large skillet over medium-high heat until hot. Add vegetable oil. Cook and stir shrimp, snow peas, bean sprouts, garlic and ginger 2 to 3 minutes or until shrimp is opaque and bean sprouts are crisp-tender.

2. Combine brown sugar, soy sauce, sesame oil, vinegar and oyster sauce in small bowl; add to skillet. Cook and stir for 1 minute or until brown sugar is dissolved.

3. Remove from heat and stir in strawberries. Serve over rice.

Makes 4 servings

Prep and Cook Time: 20 minutes

Scallops & Snow Peas

Oriental Shrimp Burritos

1 tablespoon vegetable oil
8 ounces (4 cups packed) shredded cole slaw mix with cabbage and carrots
1 teaspoon bottled minced ginger *or* 1/2 teaspoon dried ginger
1 teaspoon bottled minced garlic
1 cup bean sprouts
1/2 cup sliced green onions with tops
8 (6- or 7-inch) flour tortillas
10 to 12 ounces peeled cooked medium shrimp
1/4 cup stir-fry sauce
1/4 teaspoon dried red pepper flakes
Plum sauce or sweet and sour sauce

1. Heat oil in large, deep skillet over medium-high heat until hot. Add cole slaw mix, ginger and garlic; stir-fry 2 minutes. Add sprouts and onions; stir-fry 3 minutes.

2. While vegetable mixture is cooking, stack tortillas and wrap in wax paper. Microwave on HIGH 1 1/2 minutes or until warm.

3. Add shrimp, stir-fry sauce and pepper flakes to skillet; stir-fry 2 minutes or until heated through. Spoon about 1/3 cup shrimp mixture evenly down center of each tortilla. Fold 1 end of tortilla over filling and roll up. Serve with plum sauce. *Makes 4 servings*

Prep and Cook Time: 10 minutes

Pink Shrimp and Pineapple

1/4 cup KIKKOMAN® Stir-Fry Sauce
2 tablespoons water
2 medium zucchini
3 tablespoons vegetable oil, divided
1/2 pound medium-size raw shrimp, peeled and deveined
1 medium onion, chunked
1 teaspoon minced fresh ginger root
1 can (20 ounces) pineapple chunks in syrup, drained

Blend stir-fry sauce and water; set aside. Cut zucchini lengthwise in half, then crosswise into 1/4-inch-thick slices. Heat 1 tablespoon oil in hot wok or large skillet over high heat. Add shrimp and stir-fry 1 minute; remove. Heat remaining 2 tablespoons oil in same pan. Add zucchini, onion and ginger; stir-fry 3 minutes. Add shrimp, pineapple and stir-fry sauce mixture; cook and stir until shrimp and vegetables are coated and heated through. *Makes 4 servings*

Kitchen Snippets

To devein shrimp, cut a slit along back of shrimp and remove vein.

Oriental Shrimp Burritos

Smucker's® Mandarin Shrimp and Vegetable Stir-Fry

      1 cup SMUCKER'S® Orange
         Marmalade
      3 tablespoons soy sauce
      2 tablespoons white vinegar
      2 teaspoons hot pepper sauce
   1½ tablespoons cornstarch
      2 tablespoons vegetable oil
      1 tablespoon fresh ginger, chopped
      1 tablespoon garlic, chopped
     24 fresh jumbo shrimp, peeled and
         deveined
      1 red bell pepper, chopped
      1 yellow or green bell pepper,
         chopped
      3 cups broccoli florettes
      ½ cup water
      1 cup chopped green onions

Combine Smucker's® Orange Marmalade, soy sauce, vinegar, hot pepper sauce and cornstarch in small bowl. Stir to dissolve cornstarch and set aside.

Place large skillet or wok over high heat. Heat skillet for 1 minute, then add oil. Heat oil for 30 seconds, then add ginger, garlic and shrimp. Stir-fry for 2 to 3 minutes until shrimp begin to turn rosy pink in color. Remove shrimp; set aside.

Add peppers and broccoli to skillet and cook on high heat for 1 minute. Add water; cover and reduce heat to medium. Cook vegetables 4 to 5 minutes or until tender.

Uncover pan and increase heat to high. Add shrimp and Smucker's® Orange Marmalade mixture. Cook shrimp 2 minutes until sauce is thickened and shrimp are completely cooked. Correct seasoning with salt and fresh ground black pepper as needed.

Stir in onions and serve with boiled rice.   *Makes 4 to 6 servings*

Albacore Stir-Fry

      3 tablespoons vegetable oil
      ½ cup sliced onion
      1 clove garlic, minced or pressed
      1 bag (16 ounces) frozen Oriental
         vegetables, thawed and drained*
      1 can (12 ounces) STARKIST® Solid
         White Tuna, drained and
         chunked
      3 tablespoons soy sauce
      1 tablespoon lemon juice
      1 tablespoon water
      1 teaspoon sugar
      2 cups hot cooked rice

*May use 4 cups fresh vegetables, such as carrots, peapods, broccoli, bell peppers, mushrooms, celery and bean sprouts.

In wok or large skillet, heat oil over medium-high heat; sauté onion and garlic until onion is soft. Add vegetables; cook about 3 to 4 minutes or until vegetables are crisp-tender. Add tuna, soy sauce, lemon juice, water and sugar. Cook 1 more minute; serve over rice.   *Makes 4 servings*

Tex-Mex Stir-Fry

1 package (1.27 ounces) LAWRY'S®
Spices & Seasonings for Fajitas
¹/₃ cup water
2 tablespoons vegetable oil, divided
1¹/₂ cups broccoli flowerettes
2 carrots, thinly sliced diagonally
1 red or green bell pepper, thinly
sliced
¹/₂ cup thinly sliced celery
1 pound medium shrimp, peeled and
deveined
1¹/₂ tablespoons brown sugar
1 teaspoon ground ginger
1 teaspoon dry mustard

In small bowl, combine Spices & Seasonings for Fajitas and water; set aside. In hot large skillet or wok, add 1 tablespoon oil, broccoli, carrots, bell pepper and celery. Stir-fry 3 minutes. Remove; set aside. Add remaining 1 tablespoon oil and shrimp to same hot skillet; stir-fry 3 minutes. Add vegetables back to skillet. Pour in Spices & Seasonings for Fajitas mixture, brown sugar, ginger and mustard. Cook 2 minutes longer, tossing gently to blend.
Makes 6 servings

Serving Suggestion: Serve seafood-vegetable mixture over hot rice.

Hint: One pound thinly sliced boneless chicken or pork can be used in place of shrimp. For pork, increase cooking time an additional 1 to 2 minutes.

Louisiana Stir-Fry

2 tablespoons vegetable oil
1 pound raw medium shrimp, shelled
and deveined *or* ¹/₂ pound sea
scallops
1 bag (16 ounces) BIRDS EYE® frozen
Farm Fresh Mixtures Broccoli,
Corn & Red Peppers
¹/₂ green bell pepper, chopped
2 teaspoons water
1 can (14¹/₂ ounces) stewed
tomatoes, drained

● In wok or large skillet; heat oil over medium-high heat.

● Add shrimp; stir-fry 2 to 3 minutes or until shrimp turn pink and opaque. Remove to serving plate.

● Add vegetables, pepper and water to wok; cover and cook 4 to 6 minutes.

● Uncover; stir in tomatoes. Cook 3 to 4 minutes or until heated through and slightly thickened.

● Return shrimp to wok; cook and stir about 1 minute or until heated through.
Makes 4 servings

Variation: Substitute 1 package (16 ounces) frozen fully cooked shrimp or 1 pound imitation crab legs. Add to cooked vegetables and cook until heated through.

Prep Time: 15 minutes
Cook Time: 12 to 15 minutes

New England Clam Chowder

24 medium clams
  Salt
1 bottle (8 ounces) clam juice
3 medium potatoes, cut into
    ½-inch-thick slices
¼ teaspoon dried thyme leaves,
    crushed
¼ teaspoon ground white pepper

4 slices bacon, cut crosswise
    into ¼-inch strips
1 medium onion, chopped
⅓ cup all-purpose flour
2 cups milk
1 cup half-and-half
  Oyster crackers

1. Scrub clams with stiff brush. Soak in mixture of ⅓ cup salt to 1 gallon water 20 minutes. Drain water; repeat 2 more times. Refrigerate clams 1 hour.

2. To shuck clams, take pointed clam knife in 1 hand and thick towel or glove in the other. With towel, grip shell in palm of hand. Keeping clam level with knife, insert tip of knife between the shell next to hinge; twist to pry shell until you hear a snap. Twist to open shell, keeping clam level at all times to save juice. Cut muscle from shell and discard top shell.

3. Tip shell over strainer in bowl to catch clams; discard bottom shell. Repeat with remaining clams. Strain clam juice from bowl through triple thickness of dampened cheesecloth into small bowl; pour clam juice into 2-cup glass measure. Refrigerate until needed. Coarsely chop clams; set aside.

4. Add bottled clam juice and enough water to clam juice in glass measure to total 2 cups liquid; place liquid in Dutch oven. Add potatoes, thyme and pepper; bring to a boil. Reduce heat; simmer 15 minutes or until potatoes are tender, stirring occasionally.

5. Cook bacon in medium skillet over medium heat until almost crisp. Add onion; cook until tender but not brown. Stir flour into bacon mixture. Whisk in milk using wire whisk. Cook until mixture boils and thickens.

6. Add bacon mixture and half-and-half to potato mixture. Add clams and continue to heat until clams are firm. Serve with oyster crackers.

Makes 6 servings

New England Clam Chowder

StarKist® Vegetable Gazpacho

1 large onion, quartered
1 medium zucchini, halved lengthwise
1 yellow or crookneck squash, halved lengthwise
1 red bell pepper
1 yellow bell pepper
¾ cup bottled olive oil vinaigrette dressing
1 can (6 ounces) STARKIST® Solid White Tuna, drained and chunked
3 pounds firm ripe tomatoes, chopped
2 cucumbers, peeled, seeded and chopped
2 to 3 cloves fresh garlic, minced
½ cup fresh sourdough bread crumbs
1½ to 2 cups tomato juice

Preheat broiler. Brush onion quarters, zucchini halves, squash halves and whole peppers with dressing; reserve remaining dressing. Broil 6 to 8 minutes, turning occasionally, until vegetables are roasted and pepper skins blister and turn black. Remove from broiler. Place peppers in paper bag; close bag and let stand 15 minutes before peeling. Cool remaining vegetables. Peel skin from peppers; seed and remove membranes.

Cut roasted vegetables into large pieces; place in food processor bowl. Process until coarsely chopped. Transfer to large

bowl; add tuna, tomatoes, cucumbers, garlic, bread crumbs, 1½ cups tomato juice and remaining dressing. Blend thoroughly. Add remaining ½ cup tomato juice to thin, if necessary.

Makes 6 to 8 servings

Prep Time: 30 minutes

Shrimp Creole Stew

1½ cups raw small shrimp, shelled
1 bag (16 ounces) BIRDS EYE® frozen Farm Fresh Mixtures Broccoli, Cauliflower & Red Peppers
1 can (14½ ounces) diced tomatoes
1½ teaspoons salt
1 teaspoon hot pepper sauce
1 teaspoon vegetable oil

● In large saucepan, combine all ingredients.

● Cover; bring to boil. Reduce heat to medium-low; simmer 20 minutes or until shrimp turn opaque.

Makes 4 servings

Serving Suggestion: Serve over Spanish or white rice and with additional hot pepper sauce for added zip.

Prep Time: 5 minutes
Cook Time: 20 minutes

StarKist® Vegetable Gazpacho

GARDEN GOODNESS

Sombrero Vegetable Bake

- 1 tablespoon olive oil
- 1 clove garlic, minced
- ¼ teaspoon ground cumin
- 1 can (14½ ounces) stewed tomatoes
- 1 package (9 ounces) frozen corn, thawed
- 2 small zucchini, cut into ¾-inch chunks
- 2 tablespoons FRANK'S® Original REDHOT® Cayenne Pepper Sauce
- ¼ teaspoon salt
- 1⅓ cups FRENCH'S® French Fried Onions

Microwave Directions: Whisk together oil, garlic and cumin in 2-quart microwavable bowl. Microwave, uncovered, on HIGH 1 minute.

Stir in tomatoes with liquid, corn, zucchini, RedHot® sauce and salt. Cover tightly with plastic wrap. Microwave on HIGH 8 to 10 minutes or until zucchini is crisp-tender, stirring twice. Uncover; sprinkle with French Fried Onions. Microwave on HIGH 1 minute or until onions are golden.

Makes 6 side-dish servings

Prep Time: 10 minutes
Cook Time: 12 minutes

Sombrero Vegetable Bake

Eggplant Parmigiana

2 cups plain dry bread crumbs
1 cup (4 ounces) shredded
  ALPINE LACE® Fat Free
  Pasteurized Process Skim
  Milk Cheese Product—For
  Parmesan Lovers
2 tablespoons Italian seasoning
2 teaspoons minced garlic,
  divided
2 medium-size unpeeled
  eggplants (2 pounds), cut
  crosswise into ½-inch-thick
  slices
2 egg whites, lightly beaten
2 tablespoons olive oil, divided

1½ cups thin strips red onion
1 can (28 ounces) crushed
  tomatoes in purée,
  undrained
⅓ cup water
½ cup slivered fresh basil leaves
1 teaspoon sugar
¼ teaspoon red pepper flakes
¼ teaspoon salt
2 cups (8 ounces) shredded
  ALPINE LACE® Fat Free
  Pasteurized Process Skim
  Milk Cheese Product—For
  Mozzarella Lovers
¼ cup minced fresh parsley

1. Preheat the oven to 375°F. Spray 2 baking sheets and a 13×9×3-inch baking dish with nonstick cooking spray. In a food processor or blender, process the bread crumbs, Parmesan, Italian seasoning and 1 teaspoon of the garlic for 30 seconds. Spread on a plate.

2. Dip the eggplant slices into the egg whites, coat both sides with the crumb mixture, then arrange in a single layer on the baking sheets. Drizzle with 1 tablespoon of the oil. Bake the eggplant for 40 minutes or until crisp, turning the slices over once. Remove the eggplant from the oven and reduce the temperature to 350°F.

3. While the eggplant bakes, make the sauce: In a large skillet, heat the remaining tablespoon of the oil over medium-high heat. Add the onion and the remaining teaspoon of garlic and sauté for 5 minutes or until soft. Stir in the tomatoes and their purée, the water, basil, sugar, red pepper flakes and salt. Simmer, uncovered, for 5 minutes.

4. In the baking dish, layer a third of the eggplant slices, a third of the sauce and a third of the mozzarella cheese; repeat 2 times. Bake for 30 minutes or until bubbly; sprinkle with the parsley. *Makes 8 servings*

Nutrients per Serving: Calories 264, Total Fat 5 g, Cholesterol 12 mg

Country Corn Bake

2 cans (11 ounces each) Mexican-
    style whole kernel corn, drained*
1 can (10¾ ounces) condensed
    cream of potato soup
½ cup milk
½ cup thinly sliced celery
1⅓ cups FRENCH'S® French Fried
    Onions, divided
½ cup (2 ounces) shredded Cheddar
    cheese
2 tablespoons bacon bits**

*Or, substitute 1 bag (16 ounces) frozen whole
kernel corn, thawed and drained.

**Or, substitute 2 slices crumbled, cooked
bacon.

Preheat oven to 375°F. Combine corn,
soup, milk, celery, *⅔ cup* French Fried
Onions, cheese and bacon bits in large
bowl. Spoon mixture into 2-quart
square baking dish. Cover; bake 30
minutes or until hot and bubbly. Stir;
sprinkle with remaining *⅔ cup* onions.
Bake, uncovered, 3 minutes or until
onions are golden.

Makes 4 to 6 servings

Prep Time: 10 minutes
Cook Time: 33 minutes

Cheese Enchiladas with Green Chiles

1¼ cups (10-ounce can) ORTEGA®
    Enchilada Sauce
1 cup ORTEGA® Garden Style Salsa,
    mild
15 corn tortillas
1 pound Monterey Jack cheese,
    sliced into 3×1-inch strips,
    divided
1 can (7 ounces) ORTEGA® Whole
    Green Chiles, sliced into thirds
1 cup (4 ounces) shredded Monterey
    Jack Cheese

COMBINE enchilada sauce and salsa in
medium bowl; mix well. Pour 1½ cups
sauce mixture onto bottom of ungreased
13×9-inch baking pan.

HEAT tortillas, one at a time, in lightly
greased medium skillet over medium-
high heat for 20 seconds on each side
or until soft. Place 1 strip cheese and 1
strip chile in center of each tortilla; roll
up. Place seam-side down in baking
pan. Repeat with remaining tortillas,
cheese and chiles. Ladle remaining
sauce mixture over enchiladas; sprinkle
with shredded cheese.

BAKE, covered, in preheated 350°F.
oven for 20 minutes; remove cover.
Bake for additional 5 minutes or until
heated through and cheese is melted.

Makes 6 to 8 servings

Ratatouille Pot Pie

¼ cup olive oil
1 eggplant (about 1 pound), peeled and cut into ½-inch pieces
1 large onion, chopped
1 green or yellow bell pepper, chopped
1½ teaspoons bottled minced garlic
1 can (14½ ounces) pasta-ready diced tomatoes with garlic and herbs or Italian stewed tomatoes, undrained
1 teaspoon dried basil leaves
½ teaspoon red pepper flakes
¼ teaspoon salt
1 tablespoon balsamic vinegar
2 cups (8 ounces) shredded mozzarella cheese, divided
1 package (10 ounces) refrigerated pizza dough

1. Preheat oven to 425°F. Heat oil in large skillet over medium heat until hot. Add eggplant, onion, bell pepper and garlic. Cook 10 minutes or until eggplant begins to brown, stirring occasionally. Stir in tomatoes with juice, basil, pepper flakes and salt. Cook, uncovered, over medium-low heat 5 minutes.

2. Remove from heat; stir in vinegar. Let stand 10 minutes; stir in 1 cup cheese. Transfer mixture to ungreased 11×7-inch casserole dish. Sprinkle with remaining cheese.

3. Unroll pizza dough; arrange over top of casserole. Make decorative cut-outs using small cookie cutter, if desired. Spray dough with nonstick cooking spray. Bake 15 minutes or until crust is golden brown and vegetable mixture is bubbly. *Makes 6 servings*

Eggplant Bulgur Casserole

1 cup bulgur wheat
½ cup chopped green bell pepper
¼ cup chopped onion
¼ cup butter
4 cups cubed peeled eggplant
1 (15-ounce) can tomato sauce
1 (14½-ounce) can tomatoes, undrained, cut up
½ cup cold water
½ teaspoon dried oregano leaves, crushed
1 (8-ounce) package PHILADELPHIA BRAND® Cream Cheese, softened
1 egg
KRAFT® 100% Grated Parmesan Cheese

● Preheat oven to 350°F.

● Sauté bulgur wheat, pepper and onion in butter in large skillet until vegetables are tender. Stir in eggplant, tomato sauce, tomatoes, water and oregano. Cover; simmer 15 to 20 minutes or until eggplant is tender, stirring occasionally.

● Beat cream cheese and egg in small mixing bowl at medium speed with electric mixer until well blended.

● Place half of vegetable mixture in 1½-quart baking dish or casserole; top with cream cheese mixture and remaining vegetable mixture. Cover.

● Bake 15 minutes. Remove cover; sprinkle with Parmesan cheese. Continue baking 10 minutes or until heated. *Makes 8 to 10 servings*

Ratatouille Pot Pie

Spinach and Mushroom Enchiladas

2 packages (10 ounces each) frozen chopped spinach, thawed
1½ cups sliced mushrooms
1 can (15 ounces) pinto beans, drained and rinsed
3 teaspoons chili powder, divided
¼ teaspoon crushed red pepper
1 can (8 ounces) tomato sauce
2 tablespoons water
½ teaspoon hot pepper sauce
8 (8-inch) corn tortillas
1 cup shredded Monterey Jack cheese
Shredded lettuce (optional)
Chopped tomatoes (optional)
Light sour cream (optional)

1. Combine spinach, mushrooms, beans, 2 teaspoons chili powder and red pepper in large skillet over medium heat. Cook and stir 5 minutes; remove from heat.

2. Combine tomato sauce, water, remaining 1 teaspoon chili powder and pepper sauce in medium skillet. Dip tortillas into tomato sauce mixture; stack tortillas on waxed paper.

3. Divide spinach filling into 8 portions. Spoon onto center of tortillas; roll up and place in 11×8-inch microwavable dish. (Secure rolls with wooden picks if desired.) Spread remaining tomato sauce mixture over enchiladas.

4. Cover with vented plastic wrap. Microwave at MEDIUM (50%) 10 minutes or until heated through. Sprinkle with cheese. Microwave at MEDIUM 3 minutes or until cheese is melted. Serve with lettuce, tomatoes and sour cream. *Makes 4 servings*

Double Cheese Strata

10 to 12 slices Italian bread, about ½ inch thick
⅔ cup (about 5 ounces) sharp Cheddar light cold pack cheese food, softened
1⅓ cups FRENCH'S® French Fried Onions
1 package (10 ounces) frozen chopped broccoli, thawed and drained
½ cup (2 ounces) shredded Swiss cheese
5 eggs
3 cups milk
2 tablespoons FRENCH'S® Deli Brown Mustard
½ teaspoon salt
¼ teaspoon ground white pepper

Grease 3-quart baking dish. Spread bread slices with Cheddar cheese. Arrange slices in a single layer in bottom of prepared baking dish, pressing to fit. Layer French Fried Onions, broccoli and Swiss cheese over bread.

Beat together eggs, milk, mustard, salt and pepper in medium bowl until well blended. Pour egg mixture over layers. Let stand 10 minutes. Preheat oven to 350°F. Bake 35 minutes or until knife inserted in center comes out clean. (Cover loosely with foil near end of baking if top becomes too brown.) Cool on wire rack 10 minutes. Cut into squares to serve. *Makes 8 servings*

Prep Time: 15 minutes
Cook Time: 35 minutes
Stand Time: 10 minutes

Spinach and Mushroom Enchiladas

Ratatouille-Stuffed Pepper Halves

3 large bell peppers (1 red, 1 yellow and 1 green or any combination)
¼ cup olive oil
1 small eggplant (¾ pound), unpeeled, cut into ½-inch cubes
1 small onion, thinly sliced
1 clove garlic, minced
1 large tomato, seeded and coarsely chopped
1 cup sliced fresh mushrooms
½ teaspoon *each* dried basil and oregano leaves, crushed
½ teaspoon salt
Dash *each* black pepper and ground red pepper
1 zucchini, quartered and cut into ½-inch chunks

1. Cut peppers in half lengthwise. Scrape out seeds and membrane.

2. Place steamer basket in large saucepan; add 1 inch of water. Place peppers, cut sides up, in steamer basket; cover. Bring to a boil; steam 5 minutes or until peppers are crisp-tender. Plunge peppers into ice water to stop cooking. Place peppers in 13×9-inch baking dish.

3. Heat oil in large skillet over medium heat. Cook eggplant and onion in hot oil 10 minutes or until vegetables are soft, stirring occasionally. Add garlic, tomato, mushrooms, basil, oregano, salt, black pepper and red pepper. Bring to a boil over medium-high heat; reduce heat to medium-low. Simmer about 5 minutes, stirring occasionally. Add zucchini; simmer 5 minutes more or until mixture thickens slightly.

4. Preheat oven to 350°F. Spoon mixture evenly into peppers. Bake 15 minutes or until heated through. Garnish with plum tomato slices and fresh basil leaves, if desired.

Makes 6 side-dish servings

Viking Vegetable Cassoulet

4 cups sliced mushrooms
2 tablespoons olive oil
2 large onions, thickly sliced
1 large clove garlic, minced
2 medium zucchini, cut into 1-inch pieces
1½ cups sliced yellow squash
2 cans (16 ounces each) white beans, drained
1 can (14½ ounces) plum tomatoes, cut up, with juice
⅓ cup chopped parsley
1 teaspoon dried basil, crushed
½ teaspoon dried oregano, crushed
½ cup bread crumbs
1 teaspoon butter, melted
2 cups (8 ounces) shredded JARLSBERG Cheese

In large, deep skillet, brown mushrooms in oil. Add onions and garlic; sauté 5 minutes. Add zucchini and squash; sauté until vegetables are crisp-tender. Blend in beans, tomatoes, parsley, basil and oregano.

Spoon into 2-quart baking dish. Combine bread crumbs and butter in small bowl. Sprinkle bread crumbs around edge. Bake at 350°F 20 minutes. Top with cheese and bake 20 minutes longer. *Makes 6 to 8 servings*

Green Bean Casserole

1 can (10¾ ounces) condensed
    cream of mushroom soup
¾ cup milk
⅛ teaspoon ground black pepper
2 packages (9 ounces each)
    frozen cut green beans,
    thawed and drained *or*
    2 cans (14½ ounces each)
    cut green beans, drained

1⅓ cups FRENCH'S® French Fried
    Onions, divided

Preheat oven to 350°F. Combine soup, milk and ground pepper in 1½-quart casserole; stir until well blended. Stir in beans and ⅔ *cup* French Fried Onions.

Bake, uncovered, 30 minutes or until hot. Stir; sprinkle with remaining ⅔ *cup* onions. Bake 5 minutes or until onions are golden.

Makes 6 servings

Baked Tomato Risotto

1 jar (28 ounces) spaghetti sauce
1 can (14 ounces) chicken broth
2 cups halved sliced zucchini
1 can (4 ounces) sliced mushrooms
1 cup arborio rice
2 cups (8 ounces) shredded
    mozzarella cheese

Preheat oven to 350°F. Spray 3-quart casserole with nonstick cooking spray.

Combine spaghetti sauce, broth, zucchini, mushrooms and rice in prepared dish.

Bake, covered, 30 minutes. Remove from oven and stir casserole. Cover and bake 15 to 20 minutes more or until rice is tender. Remove from oven; sprinkle evenly with cheese. Bake, uncovered, 5 minutes or until cheese is melted.

Makes 6 servings

Lightened Up

Wild Rice, Mushroom and Spinach Skillet

⅓ cup uncooked wild rice
⅓ cup uncooked brown rice
⅓ cup uncooked long-grain white rice
1½ cups water
1 can (10½ ounces) reduced-sodium chicken broth
2 tablespoons margarine

2 cups sliced shiitake mushrooms
2 cups quartered brown mushrooms
2 cups sliced bok choy
2 cups shredded spinach
¼ cup crumbled feta cheese

1. Combine wild rice, brown rice, long-grain white rice, water and chicken broth in medium saucepan. Bring to a boil over high heat; reduce heat to low. Simmer, covered, 45 minutes or until rice is tender.

2. Melt margarine in large saucepan over medium heat. Add mushrooms; cook and stir 3 minutes. Add bok choy and spinach; cook and stir 3 minutes or until greens are wilted.

3. Add rice to greens in saucepan; stir until blended. Sprinkle with cheese just before serving. *Makes 10 servings*

Nutrients per Serving: Calories 130, Total Fat 4 g, Cholesterol 6 mg, Sodium 117 mg

Use only the caps of shiitake mushrooms and discard the tough stems.

Wild Rice, Mushroom and Spinach Skillet

Broccoli-Tofu Stir-Fry

2 cups uncooked rice
1 can (14$\frac{1}{2}$ ounces) vegetable broth, divided
3 tablespoons cornstarch
1 tablespoon reduced-sodium soy sauce
$\frac{1}{2}$ teaspoon sugar
$\frac{1}{4}$ teaspoon sesame oil
1 package (16 ounces) extra-firm tofu
1 teaspoon peanut oil
1 tablespoon minced fresh ginger
3 cloves garlic, minced
3 cups broccoli flowerets
2 cups sliced mushrooms
$\frac{1}{2}$ cup chopped green onions
1 large red bell pepper, seeded and cut into strips
  Prepared Szechuan sauce (optional)

1. Cook rice according to package directions. Combine $\frac{1}{4}$ cup vegetable broth, cornstarch, soy sauce, sugar and sesame oil in small bowl. Drain tofu and cut into 1-inch cubes.

2. Heat peanut oil in large nonstick wok or skillet over medium heat until hot. Add ginger and garlic. Cook and stir 5 minutes. Add remaining vegetable broth and broccoli, mushrooms, green onions and bell pepper. Cook and stir over medium-high heat 5 minutes or until vegetables are crisp-tender. Add tofu; cook 2 minutes, stirring occasionally. Stir cornstarch mixture; add to vegetable mixture. Cook and stir until sauce thickens. Serve over rice with Szechuan sauce.   *Makes 6 servings*

Stir-Fry Rice and Vegetables

3 tablespoons vegetable oil
1 bunch green onions, white and green parts chopped separately
1 medium sweet potato, peeled, halved lengthwise and thinly sliced
1 small green bell pepper, cut into thin strips
2 carrots, thinly sliced
1 zucchini, thinly sliced
2 cups cooked brown rice
1 cup bean sprouts
1 cup fresh mushrooms, sliced
$\frac{1}{4}$ cup honey
$\frac{1}{4}$ cup soy sauce

Heat oil in wok or large, heavy skillet over medium-high heat. Stir-fry white parts of onions, sweet potato, bell pepper, carrots and zucchini until barely tender. Add rice, sprouts, mushrooms and green onion tops. Cook quickly until heated through. If necessary, add more oil. Combine honey and soy sauce in cup. Pour over mixture and stir. Serve immediately.
          Makes 6 to 8 servings

Favorite recipe from **National Honey Board**

Broccoli-Tofu Stir-Fry

Cheesy Vegetarian Stir-Fry

2 teaspoons olive oil
3 cloves garlic, minced
1 cup thinly sliced onion
4 cups small zucchini squash, cut lengthwise in quarters, then into 1½-inch pieces
1 to 2 teaspoons dried Italian herbs
1 (9-ounce) package frozen artichoke hearts, thawed, cooked and drained (optional)
½ cup marinara sauce
½ cup shredded JARLSBERG LITE™ Cheese

Heat oil in wok over high heat; stir-fry garlic and onion 3 minutes or until lightly browned. Add zucchini and herbs; stir-fry 3 minutes or until crisp-tender. Remove from heat and stir in artichoke hearts, marinara sauce and cheese. Serve with cannellini beans or over pasta such as orrechiette or linguine.   *Makes 4 to 6 servings*

Vegetarian Tofu Stir-Fry

1 block tofu
2 tablespoons vegetable oil
1 teaspoon minced fresh gingerroot
1 medium onion, chunked
⅛ teaspoon salt
6 ounces fresh snow peas, trimmed and cut diagonally in half
⅓ cup KIKKOMAN® Stir-Fry Sauce
2 medium-size fresh tomatoes, chunked
¼ cup slivered blanched almonds, toasted

Cut tofu into ½-inch cubes; drain well on several layers of paper towels. Heat oil in hot wok or large skillet over high heat. Add ginger; stir-fry 30 seconds, or until fragrant. Add onion and salt; stir-fry 2 minutes. Add snow peas; stir-fry 1 minute. Add stir-fry sauce, tomatoes and tofu. Gently stir to coat tofu and vegetables with sauce. Reduce heat and cook only until tomatoes and tofu are heated through. Sprinkle with almonds; serve immediately.

Makes 4 servings

Creamy Cheddar Cheese Soup

2 cans (10¾ ounces each) condensed Cheddar cheese soup
3 cups milk or water
3 cups cooked vegetables, such as cauliflower, carrots and asparagus, cut into bite-size pieces
2 cups cooked medium shell pasta
1⅓ cups FRENCH'S® French Fried Onions

Combine soup and milk in large saucepan. Stir in vegetables and pasta. Bring to a boil. Reduce heat. Cook until heated through, stirring often.

Place French Fried Onions on microwavable dish. Microwave on HIGH 1 minute or until onions are golden.

Ladle soup into individual bowls. Sprinkle with French Fried Onions.

Makes 6 servings

Prep Time: 10 minutes
Cook Time: 5 minutes

Cheesy Polenta with Zucchini Stew

2¼ cups water, divided
1 cup stone-ground or regular yellow cornmeal
2 eggs
2 egg whites
¾ cup reduced-fat sharp Cheddar cheese
1 jalapeño pepper, minced*
1 teaspoon margarine
½ teaspoon salt, divided
1 tablespoon olive oil
1 cup chopped onion
2 cups coarsely chopped peeled eggplant
3 cloves minced garlic
3 cups chopped zucchini
1 cup chopped tomato
½ cup chopped yellow bell pepper
2 tablespoons minced fresh parsley
1 tablespoon minced fresh oregano
¼ teaspoon minced fresh rosemary
¼ teaspoon crushed red pepper
¼ teaspoon freshly ground pepper blend

*Jalapeño peppers can sting and irritate the skin; wear rubber gloves when handling peppers and do not touch your eyes. Wash hands after handling jalapeño peppers.

1. Bring 2 cups water to a boil. Slowly add cornmeal, stirring constantly. Bring to a boil, stirring constantly, until mixture thickens. Lightly beat eggs and egg whites with remaining ¼ cup water. Add to cornmeal; cook and stir until bubbly. Remove from heat; stir in cheese, jalapeño pepper, margarine and ¼ teaspoon salt. Pour into 9-inch square baking pan. Cover and refrigerate several hours or until firm.

2. Heat olive oil in medium saucepan over medium heat until hot. Cook and stir onion, eggplant and garlic 5 minutes or until onion is transparent. Add zucchini, tomato, bell pepper, parsley, oregano, rosemary, remaining ¼ teaspoon salt, red pepper and pepper blend. Simmer, uncovered, 1 hour.

3. Spray large nonstick skillet with nonstick vegetable cooking spray. Heat skillet over medium heat until hot. Cut polenta in 6 rectangles. Cook over medium heat 8 minutes on each side or until lightly browned. Serve stew over polenta. *Makes 6 servings*

Blender Potato Soup

½ cup WESSON® Vegetable Oil
3 cups chopped celery
1½ cups chopped onions
1 teaspoon fresh minced garlic
1 quart chicken broth
3 cups peeled and diced russet potatoes
½ cup chopped fresh parsley
½ teaspoon salt
¼ teaspoon pepper
Shredded sharp Cheddar cheese

In a large saucepan, heat Wesson Oil. Add celery, onions and garlic; sauté until tender. Stir in remaining ingredients except ⅓ cup parsley and cheese; bring to a boil and reduce heat. Simmer, covered, for 20 minutes or until potatoes are tender. Pour half of mixture into blender; purée until smooth. Set aside. Pour remaining soup into blender; blend until coarsely chopped. Combine both mixtures. Garnish with remaining parsley and cheese. *Makes 8 servings*

Jamaican Black Bean Stew

2 cups brown rice
2 pounds sweet potatoes
3 pounds butternut squash
1 large onion, coarsely chopped
1 can (about 14 ounces) vegetable broth
3 cloves garlic, minced
1 tablespoon curry powder
1½ teaspoons allspice
½ teaspoon ground red pepper
¼ teaspoon salt
2 cans (15 ounces each) black beans, drained and rinsed
½ cup raisins
3 tablespoons fresh lime juice
1 cup diced tomato
1 cup diced, peeled cucumber

1. Prepare rice according to package directions. Peel sweet potatoes; cut into ¾-inch chunks to measure 4 cups. Peel squash; remove seeds. Cut flesh into ¾-inch cubes to measure 5 cups.

2. Combine potatoes, squash, onion, broth, garlic, curry powder, allspice, pepper and salt in Dutch oven. Bring to a boil; reduce heat to low. Simmer, covered, 5 minutes. Add beans and raisins. Simmer 5 minutes or just until sweet potatoes and squash are tender and beans are hot. Remove from heat; stir in lime juice.

3. Serve stew over brown rice and top with tomato and cucumber.

Makes 8 servings

Curried Vegetable-Rice Soup

1 package (16 ounces) frozen vegetable medley, such as broccoli, cauliflower, sugar snap peas and red bell peppers
1 can (about 14 ounces) vegetable broth
¾ cup uncooked instant brown rice
2 teaspoons curry powder
½ teaspoon salt
½ teaspoon hot pepper sauce or to taste
1 can (14 ounces) unsweetened coconut milk
1 tablespoon fresh lime juice

1. Combine vegetables and broth in large saucepan. Cover; bring to a boil over high heat. Stir in rice, curry powder, salt and pepper sauce; reduce heat to medium-low. Cover and simmer 8 minutes or until rice is tender, stirring once.

2. Stir in coconut milk; cook 3 minutes or until heated through. Remove from heat. Stir in lime juice. Ladle into shallow bowls and serve immediately.

Makes 4 servings

Prep and Cook Time: 16 minutes

Jamaican Black Bean Stew

Southwestern Two Bean Chili & Rice

1 bag (about ½ cup uncooked) boil-in-bag white rice
1 tablespoon vegetable oil
1 cup chopped onion
1 cup chopped green bell pepper
1½ teaspoons bottled minced garlic
1 can (15½ ounces) chili beans in spicy or mild sauce, undrained
1 can (15½ ounces) black or pinto beans, drained
1 can (10 ounces) diced tomatoes with green chilies, undrained
1 tablespoon chili powder
2 teaspoons ground cumin
1 cup (4 ounces) shredded Cheddar or Monterey Jack cheese

1. Cook rice according to package directions.

2. While rice is cooking, heat oil in large saucepan over medium-high heat until hot. Add onion, bell pepper and garlic. Cook 5 minutes, stirring occasionally. Stir in chili beans with sauce, black beans, tomatoes with juice, chili powder and cumin. Cover; bring to a boil over high heat. Reduce heat to medium-low. Simmer, covered, 10 minutes.

3. Transfer rice to 4 shallow bowls. Ladle bean mixture over rice; top with cheese.   *Makes 4 servings*

Prep and Cook Time: 20 minutes

Hearty Minestrone Soup

2 cans (10¾ ounces each) condensed Italian tomato soup
3 cups water
3 cups cooked vegetables, such as zucchini, peas, corn or beans
2 cups cooked ditalini pasta
1⅓ cups FRENCH'S® French Fried Onions

Combine soup and water in large saucepan. Add vegetables and pasta. Bring to a boil. Reduce heat. Cook until heated through, stirring often.

Place French Fried Onions in microwavable dish. Microwave on HIGH 1 minute or until onions are golden.

Ladle soup into individual bowls. Sprinkle with French Fried Onions.
                Makes 6 servings

Ditalini pasta are very short tubes of macaroni.

Southwestern Two Bean Chili & Rice

Vegetable Soup with Delicious Dumplings

SOUP

> 2 tablespoons WESSON® Vegetable Oil
> 1 cup diced onion
> ¾ cup sliced celery
> 7 cups homemade chicken broth *or* 4 (14½-ounce) cans chicken broth
> 2 (14.5-ounce) cans HUNT'S® Stewed Tomatoes
> ½ teaspoon garlic powder
> ½ teaspoon salt
> ½ teaspoon fines herbs seasoning
> ⅛ teaspoon pepper
> 1 (16-ounce) bag frozen mixed vegetables
> 1 (15½-ounce) can HUNT'S® Red Kidney Beans, drained
> ⅓ cup uncooked long-grain rice

DUMPLINGS

> 2 cups all-purpose flour
> 3 tablespoons baking powder
> 1 teaspoon salt
> ⅔ cup milk
> ⅓ cup WESSON® Vegetable Oil
> 1½ teaspoons chopped fresh parsley

Soup

In a large Dutch oven, heat Wesson Oil. Add onion and celery; sauté until crisp-tender. Stir in next 6 ingredients, ending with pepper; bring to a boil. Add vegetables, beans and rice. Reduce heat; cover and simmer 15 to 20 minutes or until rice is cooked and vegetables are tender.

Dumplings

Meanwhile, in a medium bowl, combine flour, baking powder and salt; blend well. Add milk, Wesson Oil and parsley; mix until batter forms a ball in the bowl. Drop dough by rounded tablespoons into simmering soup. Cook, covered, 10 minutes; remove lid and cook an additional 10 minutes.

Makes 10 servings

Veggie Soup

> 1 bag (16 ounces) BIRDS EYE® frozen Mixed Vegetables
> 1 can (11 ounces) tomato rice soup
> 1 can (10 ounces) French onion soup
> 1 soup can of water

• In large saucepan, cook vegetables according to package directions; drain.

• Add both cans of soup and water; cook over medium-high heat until heated through.

Makes 4 servings

Serving Suggestion: Sprinkle individual servings evenly with 1 cup shredded Cheddar cheese.

Prep Time: 2 minutes
Cook Time: 10 to 12 minutes

Vegetable Soup with Delicious Dumplings

Lightened Up

Vegetable-Bean Chowder

Nonstick cooking spray
½ cup chopped onion
½ cup chopped celery
2 cups water
½ teaspoon salt
2 cups cubed peeled potatoes
1 cup carrot slices
1 can (15 ounces) cream-style corn

1 can (15 ounces) cannellini beans or navy beans, drained and rinsed
¼ teaspoon dried tarragon leaves
¼ teaspoon ground black pepper
2 cups low-fat (1%) milk
2 tablespoons cornstarch

1. Spray 4-quart Dutch oven or large saucepan with nonstick cooking spray; heat over medium heat until hot. Add onion and celery. Cook and stir 3 minutes or until crisp-tender.

2. Add water and salt. Bring to a boil over high heat. Add potatoes and carrot. Reduce heat to medium. Simmer, covered, 10 minutes or until potatoes and carrot are tender.

3. Stir in corn, beans, tarragon and pepper. Simmer, covered, 10 minutes or until heated through.

4. Stir milk into cornstarch in medium bowl until smooth. Stir into vegetable mixture. Simmer, uncovered, until thickened.   *Makes 5 (1½-cup) servings*

Nutrients per Serving: Calories 273, Total Fat 2 g, Cholesterol 4 mg, Sodium 696 mg

Spinach and Mushroom Soup

1½ cups 1% milk
3 medium potatoes, peeled and chopped (1 cup)
1 box (10 ounces) BIRDS EYE® frozen Chopped Spinach
1 can (10¾ ounces) cream of mushroom soup

• In large saucepan, heat milk and potatoes over medium-low heat 10 minutes.

• Add spinach and soup.

• Cook about 10 minutes or until soup begins to bubble and potatoes are tender, stirring frequently.

Makes 4 servings

Vegetable-Bean Chowder

PASTA PERFECTION

Country Sausage Macaroni and Cheese

- **1 pound BOB EVANS® Special Seasonings Roll Sausage**
- **1½ cups milk**
- **12 ounces pasteurized processed Cheddar cheese, cut into cubes**
- **½ cup Dijon mustard**
- **1 cup diced fresh or drained canned tomatoes**
- **1 cup sliced mushrooms**
- **⅓ cup sliced green onions**
- **⅛ teaspoon cayenne pepper**
- **12 ounces uncooked elbow macaroni**
- **2 tablespoons Parmesan cheese**

Preheat oven to 350°F. Crumble and cook sausage in medium skillet until browned. Drain on paper towels. Combine milk, cheese and mustard in medium saucepan; cook and stir over low heat until cheese melts and mixture is smooth. Stir in sausage, tomatoes, mushrooms, green onions and cayenne pepper. Remove from heat.

Cook macaroni according to package directions; drain. Combine hot macaroni and cheese mixture in large bowl; toss until well coated. Spoon into greased 2-quart casserole dish. Cover and bake 15 to 20 minutes. Stir; sprinkle with Parmesan cheese. Bake, uncovered, 5 minutes more. Let stand 10 minutes before serving. Refrigerate leftovers. *Makes 6 to 8 servings*

Country Sausage Macaroni and Cheese

Chicken Primavera Buffet

     12 ounces uncooked thin spaghetti
      ¼ cup prepared pesto
      ¼ cup prepared fat-free Italian salad
          dressing
      ½ teaspoon crushed red pepper
       2 cups water
       1 cup thinly sliced carrots
       1 cup broccoli flowerets
       1 cup pea pods
       1 can (4 ounces) sliced water
           chestnuts, drained
           Nonstick cooking spray
       8 boneless skinless chicken breast
           halves

1. Preheat oven to 350°F. Cook pasta according to package directions, omitting salt. Drain and rinse well under cold water until pasta is cool; drain well. Place in large bowl; set aside.

2. Combine pesto, Italian dressing and pepper in small bowl. Reserve 1 tablespoon pesto mixture. Add remaining pesto mixture to pasta; toss to coat well.

3. In large saucepan, bring water to a boil over high heat. Add carrots, broccoli and pea pods; cook 3 minutes. Drain vegetables. Add water chestnuts and vegetables to pasta; toss to blend well. Spray 13×9-inch baking pan with nonstick cooking spray. Transfer pasta and vegetables to baking pan.

4. Spray large nonstick skillet with cooking spray; heat over medium heat until hot. Add chicken; cook until browned on both sides. Cover; cook 10 minutes or until no longer pink in center and juices run clear. Place chicken on pasta and vegetables. Pour juices from skillet over chicken. Spread reserved pesto mixture over chicken. Bake 45 minutes or until heated through.   *Makes 8 servings*

Pizza Hot Dish

    1½ to 2 pounds ground beef
      ¼ cup chopped onion
       1 package (10 ounces) egg noodles
       2 jars (15½ ounces each) pizza
           sauce
       1 can (10¾ ounces) condensed
           Cheddar cheese soup
       2 cups (8 ounces) shredded
           mozzarella cheese

1. In large skillet brown ground beef with onion. Drain.

2. Prepare egg noodles according to package directions.

3. Add sauce, soup and cooked egg noodles to ground beef; mix well. Spoon into 13×9-inch baking pan or large casserole. Bake at 350°F for 30 minutes. Sprinkle with mozzarella cheese and bake an additional 15 minutes.   *Makes 8 to 12 servings*

Favorite recipe from **North Dakota Beef Commission**

Chicken Primavera Buffet

Tuna Noodle Casserole

1 can (10¾ ounces) condensed
   cream of mushroom soup
1 cup milk
3 cups hot cooked rotini pasta
   (2 cups uncooked)
1 can (12.5 ounces) tuna packed
   in water, drained and flaked

1⅓ cups FRENCH'S® French Fried
   Onions, divided
1 package (10 ounces) frozen
   peas and carrots
½ cup (2 ounces) shredded
   Cheddar or grated Parmesan
   cheese

Combine soup and milk in 2-quart microwavable shallow casserole. Stir in pasta, tuna, ⅔ *cup* French Fried Onions, vegetables and cheese. Cover; microwave on HIGH 10 minutes* or until heated through, stirring halfway through cooking time. Top with remaining ⅔ *cup* onions. Microwave 1 minute or until onions are golden. *Makes 6 servings*

*Or, bake, covered, in 350°F oven 25 to 30 minutes.

Cheese Stuffed Shells with Basil

1 cup (8 ounces) low-fat ricotta
   cheese
1 (8-ounce) package HEALTHY
   CHOICE® Fat Free natural
   shredded Mozzarella Cheese
1 cup chopped fresh basil
2 teaspoons minced fresh garlic
6 ounces (16 shells) jumbo pasta
   shells, cooked
1 (26-ounce) jar HEALTHY CHOICE®
   Pasta Sauce

Heat oven to 350°F. In large bowl, stir together ricotta cheese, 1 cup mozzarella cheese, basil and garlic. Fill each shell with about 2 tablespoons cheese filling. Place in 12×7-inch baking dish sprayed with nonstick cooking spray. Pour sauce over filled shells. Sprinkle with remaining mozzarella cheese. Cover and bake at 350°F, 20 to 25 minutes.

Makes 8 servings

Tuna Noodle Casserole

Turkey Cazuela

8 ounces uncooked linguini, broken in half*
1⅓ cups FRENCH'S® French Fried Onions, divided
2 cups (10 ounces) cubed cooked turkey
1 can (10¾ ounces) condensed cream of chicken soup
1 jar (8 ounces) picante sauce
½ cup sour cream
1 cup (4 ounces) shredded Cheddar cheese

*Or, substitute 4 cups cooked pasta for uncooked linguini.

Preheat oven to 350°F. Grease 2-quart shallow baking dish. Cook linguini according to package directions, using shortest cooking time. Layer linguini, ⅔ *cup* French Fried Onions and turkey in prepared baking dish.

Combine soup, picante sauce and sour cream in large bowl. Pour over turkey.

Cover; bake 40 minutes or until hot and bubbling. Stir gently. Sprinkle with cheese and remaining ⅔ *cup* onions. Bake 5 minutes or until onions are golden.   *Makes 4 to 6 servings*

Prep Time: 20 minutes
Cook Time: 45 minutes

Pasta with Salmon and Dill

6 ounces uncooked mafalda
1 tablespoon olive oil
2 ribs celery, sliced
1 small red onion, chopped
1 can (10¾ ounces) condensed cream of celery soup, undiluted
¼ cup reduced-fat mayonnaise
¼ cup dry white wine
3 tablespoons chopped fresh parsley
1 teaspoon dried dill weed
1 can (7½ ounces) pink salmon, drained
½ cup dry bread crumbs
1 tablespoon margarine or butter, melted
Fresh dill sprigs (optional)

Preheat oven to 350°F. Spray 1-quart square baking dish with nonstick cooking spray.

Cook pasta according to package directions until al dente; drain and set aside.

Meanwhile, heat oil in medium skillet over medium-high heat until hot. Add celery and onion; cook and stir 2 minutes or until vegetables are tender. Set aside.

Combine soup, mayonnaise, wine, parsley and dill weed in large bowl. Stir in pasta, vegetables and salmon until pasta is well coated. Pour salmon mixture into prepared dish.

Combine bread crumbs and margarine in small bowl; sprinkle evenly over casserole.

Bake, uncovered, 25 minutes or until hot and bubbly. Garnish with dill sprigs, if desired.   *Makes 4 servings*

Lightened Up

Trim Turkey Tetrazzini

½ pound BUTTERBALL® Oven
    Roasted Turkey Breast, sliced
    ½ inch thick in the deli,
    cubed
½ pound uncooked spaghetti,
    broken
¼ cup butter or margarine
¼ cup flour
1 can (14½ ounces) fat free
    reduced sodium chicken
    broth

2¾ cups milk
½ teaspoon salt
¼ teaspoon ground white pepper
8 ounces fresh mushrooms,
    sliced
¼ cup shredded Parmesan cheese
½ cup crumbled salad croutons

Cook and drain spaghetti. Melt butter in large skillet over medium heat. Whisk in flour. Add chicken broth, milk, salt and pepper. Heat, stirring constantly, until thickened. Add turkey, mushrooms, Parmesan cheese and spaghetti to skillet. Spray 13×9-inch baking dish with nonstick cooking spray. Pour turkey mixture into baking dish. Top with crumbled croutons. Bake 30 to 40 minutes in preheated 350°F oven. *Makes 8 servings*

Nutrients per Serving: Calories 200, Total Fat 8 g, Sodium 700 mg

Baked Ziti with Walnuts

1 cup uncooked ziti pasta
1 box (10 ounces) BIRDS EYE® frozen
    Peas & Pearl Onions
1 cup tomato sauce
½ cup chopped walnuts
1 tablespoon olive oil
2 tablespoons grated Parmesan
    cheese

• Preheat oven to 350°F.

• Cook ziti according to package directions; drain and set aside.

• In large bowl, combine vegetables, tomato sauce, walnuts and oil. Add ziti; toss well.

• Place mixture in 13×9-inch baking pan. Sprinkle with cheese.

• Bake 20 minutes or until heated through. *Makes 4 servings*

Prep Time: 10 minutes
Cook Time: 20 minutes

Penne, Sausage & Ham Casserole

1 pound HILLSHIRE FARM® Smoked Sausage, cut into ½-inch slices
4 ounces HILLSHIRE FARM® Ham, cubed
2 cups milk
2 tablespoons all-purpose flour
8 ounces uncooked penne pasta, cooked and drained
2½ cups (10 ounces) shredded mozzarella cheese
⅓ cup grated Parmesan cheese
1 jar (16 ounces) prepared pasta sauce
⅓ cup bread crumbs

Preheat oven to 350°F.

Lightly brown Smoked Sausage and Ham in large skillet over medium heat. Stir in milk and flour; bring to a boil, stirring constantly. Stir in pasta and cheeses. Pour sausage mixture into small casserole; pour pasta sauce over top. Bake, covered, 25 minutes. Uncover and sprinkle with bread crumbs; place under broiler to brown topping. *Makes 4 servings*

Angel Hair Mornay

1 package (16 ounces) angel hair pasta (capellini)
1 teaspoon olive oil
1 box (10 ounces) BIRDS EYE® frozen Deluxe Broccoli Florets
1 box (10 ounces) BIRDS EYE® frozen Cauliflower with Cheese Sauce

● Preheat oven to 350°F.

● In large saucepan, cook pasta according to package directions; drain.

● Combine pasta, oil and broccoli in 13×9-inch baking pan.

● Cover with cauliflower/cheese sauce mixture. Bake 20 minutes or until heated through. *Makes 4 servings*

Prep Time: 10 minutes
Cook Time: 20 minutes

Ham-Noodle Casserole

1 can (10¾ ounces) condensed Cheddar cheese soup, undiluted
½ cup milk
½ cup sour cream
½ cup sliced celery
1 can (2½ ounces) sliced mushrooms, drained
2 cups diced HILLSHIRE FARM® Ham
3 ounces uncooked medium-size noodles, cooked and drained
¾ cup crushed rich round crackers
1 tablespoon butter or margarine, melted

Preheat oven to 375°F.

Combine soup, milk and sour cream in large bowl. Add celery and mushrooms. Stir in Ham and noodles. Pour mixture into medium casserole. Combine cracker crumbs and butter in small bowl; sprinkle over ham mixture. Bake, uncovered, 30 minutes or until hot and bubbly. *Makes 6 servings*

Penne, Sausage & Ham Casserole

Creamy Chicken and Pasta with Spinach

6 ounces uncooked egg noodles
1 tablespoon olive oil
¼ cup chopped onion
¼ cup chopped red bell pepper
1 package (10 ounces) frozen spinach, thawed and drained
2 boneless skinless chicken breast halves (¾ pound), cooked and cut into 1-inch pieces
1 can (4 ounces) sliced mushrooms, drained
2 cups (8 ounces) shredded Swiss cheese
1 container (8 ounces) sour cream
¾ cup half-and-half
2 eggs, slightly beaten
½ teaspoon salt
    Red onion and fresh spinach for garnish

Preheat oven to 350°F. Prepare egg noodles according to package directions; set aside.

Heat oil in large skillet over medium-high heat. Add onion and bell pepper; cook and stir 2 minutes or until onion is tender. Add spinach, chicken, mushrooms and cooked noodles; stir to combine.

Combine cheese, sour cream, half-and-half, eggs and salt in medium bowl; blend well.

Add cheese mixture to chicken mixture; stir to combine. Pour into 13×9-inch baking dish coated with nonstick cooking spray. Bake covered 30 to 35 minutes or until heated through. Garnish with red onion and fresh spinach, if desired.

Makes 8 servings

Rotini & Ham Bake

1 can (10¾ ounces) condensed cream of celery soup, undiluted
1 cup milk
1 cup (4 ounces) shredded Cheddar cheese, divided
¼ teaspoon salt
¼ teaspoon onion powder
¼ teaspoon garlic powder
¼ teaspoon black pepper
2 cups cooked rotini pasta
1½ cups cubed HILLSHIRE FARM® Ham
1 head broccoli, divided into spears and cooked

Preheat oven to 350°F.

Combine soup, milk, ½ cup cheese, salt, onion powder, garlic powder and pepper in medium bowl; set aside. Combine pasta and Ham in medium baking dish. Arrange broccoli spears around top of dish, pushing spears into pasta mixture. Pour soup mixture evenly over top of pasta mixture. Bake, covered, 35 minutes. Top with remaining ½ cup cheese. Bake, uncovered, 5 minutes or until cheese has melted.   *Makes 4 to 6 servings*

Creamy Chicken and Pasta with Spinach

Creamy SPAM™ Broccoli Casserole

Nonstick cooking spray
1 (7-ounce) package elbow macaroni
2 cups frozen cut broccoli, thawed and drained
1 (12-ounce) can SPAM® Lite Luncheon Meat, cubed
½ cup chopped red bell pepper
2 cups skim milk
2 tablespoons cornstarch
¼ teaspoon black pepper
1 cup (4 ounces) shredded fat-free Cheddar cheese
¾ cup soft bread crumbs
2 teaspoons margarine, melted

Heat oven to 350°F. Spray 2-quart casserole with nonstick cooking spray. Cook macaroni according to package directions; drain. In prepared casserole, combine macaroni, broccoli, SPAM® and bell pepper. In small saucepan, stir together milk, cornstarch and black pepper until cornstarch is dissolved. Bring to a boil, stirring constantly, until thickened. Reduce heat to low. Add cheese; stir until melted. Stir sauce into SPAM™ mixture. Combine bread crumbs and margarine; sprinkle on top of casserole. Bake 40 minutes or until thoroughly heated.

Makes 8 servings

Turkey Tetrazzini

½ pound fresh mushrooms, sliced
¼ cup sliced green onions
1 tablespoon margarine
2 tablespoons all-purpose flour
¼ teaspoon black pepper
1 (12-ounce) can light evaporated skim milk
⅓ cup low-sodium chicken broth
2 tablespoons sherry (optional)
8 ounces spaghetti
1 (8-ounce) package HEALTHY CHOICE® Fat Free natural shredded Mozzarella Cheese
1 pound turkey breast, cooked, cut into strips

Heat oven to 375°F. Cook mushrooms and green onions in margarine, stirring occasionally, until mushrooms are tender, about 7 minutes. Stir in flour and pepper. Cook and stir 1 minute. Add evaporated milk, chicken broth and sherry. Cook, stirring occasionally until sauce is thickened. Remove from heat. Cook spaghetti according to package directions. Drain, rinse and keep spaghetti warm. In 2-quart casserole sprayed with nonstick cooking spray, layer half of cooked spaghetti, cheese, turkey strips and sauce. Repeat layers with remaining ingredients. Bake at 375°F for 25 to 30 minutes or until bubbly and hot.   *Makes 6 servings*

Creamy SPAM™ Broccoli Casserole

Cheese-Sauced Manicotti

     8 manicotti shells
     1 cup chopped onion
 ¼ cup water
     2 cloves garlic, minced
     3 tablespoons all-purpose flour
1²/₃ cups fat-free (skim) milk, divided
  **¾ cup shredded part-skim mozzarella
          cheese**
     1 teaspoon dried Italian seasoning
 ¼ teaspoon ground black pepper
     **1 package (10 ounces) frozen
          chopped spinach, thawed and
          well drained**
     1 cup nonfat ricotta cheese
 ½ cup 1% low-fat cottage cheese
 ½ teaspoon dried marjoram leaves
     1 medium tomato, sliced

Prepare manicotti according to package directions; drain. Rinse under cold water; drain.

Meanwhile, preheat oven to 350°F. Coat 13×9-inch baking dish with nonstick cooking spray.

Combine onion, water and garlic in medium saucepan. Bring to a boil over high heat. Reduce heat to medium-low. Cover; simmer 3 to 4 minutes or until onion is tender. Blend flour and ⅓ cup milk in small bowl until smooth. Stir into onion mixture. Stir in remaining 1⅓ cups milk. Cook and stir over medium heat until mixture boils and thickens. Cook and stir 1 minute. Add mozzarella cheese, Italian seasoning and pepper. Cook and stir until cheese melts.

Combine spinach, ricotta cheese, cottage cheese, marjoram and ⅓ cup sauce in medium bowl. Spoon ⅓ cup spinach mixture into each manicotti shell. Place in prepared baking dish. Pour remaining sauce over top. Cover; bake 30 to 35 minutes or until heated through. Arrange tomato slices on top. Bake, uncovered, 4 to 5 minutes or until tomato is heated through.

Makes 4 servings

Monterey Spaghetti Casserole

     4 ounces uncooked spaghetti
     1 egg, beaten
     1 cup sour cream
     **2 cups (8 ounces) shredded
          Monterey Jack cheese**
 ¼ cup grated Parmesan cheese
     **1 package (10 ounces) frozen
          chopped spinach, thawed and
          drained**
**1⅓ cups FRENCH'S® French Fried
          Onions, divided**

Preheat oven to 350°F. Cook spaghetti according to package directions using shortest cooking time. Drain.

Combine egg and sour cream in 8-inch square baking dish. Stir in spaghetti, cheeses, spinach and ⅔ cup French Fried Onions.

Cover; bake 30 minutes or until heated through. Stir. Top with remaining ⅔ cup onions. Bake, uncovered, 5 minutes or until onions are golden.

Makes 4 servings

Prep Time: 10 minutes
Cook Time: 35 minutes

Chicken and Veggie Lasagna

    Tomato-Herb Sauce (recipe follows)
    Nonstick olive oil cooking spray
1½ cups thinly sliced zucchini
  1 cup thinly sliced carrots
  3 cups torn fresh spinach leaves
 ½ teaspoon salt
  1 package (15 ounces) fat-free ricotta cheese
 ½ cup grated Parmesan cheese
  9 lasagna noodles, cooked and drained
  2 cups (8 ounces) reduced-fat shredded mozzarella cheese

1. Prepare Tomato-Herb Sauce.

2. Preheat oven to 350°F. Spray large nonstick skillet with cooking spray; heat over medium heat until hot. Add zucchini and carrots; cook and stir about 5 minutes or until almost tender. Remove from heat; stir in spinach and salt.

3. Combine ricotta and Parmesan cheese in small bowl. Spread 1⅔ cups Tomato-Herb Sauce on bottom of 13×9-inch baking pan. Top with 3 noodles. Spoon half the ricotta cheese mixture over noodles; spread lightly with spatula. Spoon half the zucchini mixture over ricotta cheese mixture; sprinkle with 1 cup mozzarella cheese. Repeat layers; place remaining 3 noodles on top.

4. Spread remaining Tomato-Herb Sauce over noodles. Cover with aluminum foil; bake 1 hour or until sauce is bubbly. Let stand 5 to 10 minutes; cut into rectangles. Garnish as desired. *Makes 12 servings*

Tomato-Herb Sauce

    Nonstick olive oil cooking spray
1½ cups chopped onions (about 2 medium)
  4 cloves garlic, minced
  1 tablespoon dried basil leaves
  1 teaspoon dried oregano leaves
 ½ teaspoon dried tarragon leaves
 ¼ teaspoon dried thyme leaves
2½ pounds ripe tomatoes, peeled and cut into wedges
  1 pound ground chicken, cooked, crumbled and drained
 ¾ cup water
 ¼ cup no-salt-added tomato paste
 ½ teaspoon salt
 ½ teaspoon pepper

1. Spray large nonstick skillet with cooking spray; heat over medium heat until hot. Add onions, garlic, basil, oregano, tarragon and thyme; cook and stir about 5 minutes or until onions are tender.

2. Add tomatoes, chicken, water and tomato paste; heat to a boil. Reduce heat to low and simmer, uncovered, about 20 minutes or until sauce is reduced to 5 cups. Stir in salt and pepper. *Makes 5 cups*

Chicken Parmesan Noodle Bake

1 package (12 ounces) extra-wide noodles
4 boneless, skinless chicken breast halves
¼ teaspoon rosemary, crushed
2 cans (14½ ounces *each*) DEL MONTE® Italian Recipe Stewed Tomatoes
½ cup (2 ounces) shredded mozzarella cheese
¼ cup (1 ounce) grated Parmesan cheese

1. Preheat oven to 450°F.

2. Cook noodles according to package directions; drain.

3. Meanwhile, sprinkle chicken with rosemary; season with salt and pepper, if desired. Arrange chicken in 13×9-inch baking dish. Bake, uncovered, 20 minutes or until chicken is no longer pink in center. Drain; remove chicken from dish.

4. Drain tomatoes, reserving liquid. In large bowl, toss reserved liquid with noodles; place in baking dish. Top with chicken and tomatoes; sprinkle with cheeses.

5. Bake 10 minutes or until heated through. Sprinkle with additional Parmesan cheese and garnish, if desired.
Makes 4 servings

Prep and Cook Time: 35 minutes

Alfredo Pasta Swirls

4 ounces uncooked fettuccini pasta
1 package (10 ounces) frozen peas and carrots, thawed and drained
1 package (10 ounces) frozen cauliflower florets, thawed and drained
1 cup (4 ounces) shredded mozzarella cheese
1⅓ cups FRENCH'S® French Fried Onions, divided
1 container (10 ounces) refrigerated Alfredo sauce
½ cup milk
⅓ cup grated Parmesan cheese

Preheat oven to 375°F. Prepare pasta according to package directions using shortest cooking time. Drain; keep warm.

Combine vegetables, mozzarella cheese and ⅔ *cup* French Fried Onions in 2-quart oblong baking dish. Twirl few strands of warm fettuccini around long-tined fork to form pasta swirl. Remove pasta swirl from fork; stand upright on top of vegetable layer. Repeat to form 5 more swirls.

Combine Alfredo sauce and milk in medium bowl. Pour over pasta and vegetables. Cover loosely with foil; bake 35 minutes or until heated through. Gently stir sauce and vegetables around pasta. Top with Parmesan cheese. Sprinkle remaining ⅔ *cup* onions around pasta. Bake, uncovered, 3 minutes or until onions are golden.   *Makes 6 servings*

Prep Time: 15 minutes
Cook Time: 38 minutes

Chicken Parmesan Noodle Bake

Chicken-Asparagus Casserole

2 teaspoons vegetable oil
1 cup seeded and chopped green and/or red bell peppers
1 medium onion, chopped
2 cloves garlic, minced
1 can (10¾ ounces) condensed cream of asparagus soup
2 eggs
1 container (8 ounces) ricotta cheese
2 cups (8 ounces) shredded Cheddar cheese, divided
1½ cups chopped cooked chicken, cut into ½-inch pieces
1 package (10 ounces) frozen chopped asparagus,* thawed and drained
8 ounces egg noodles, cooked
Ground black pepper (optional)

*Or, substitute ½ pound fresh asparagus cut into ½-inch pieces. Bring 6 cups water to a boil over high heat in large saucepan. Add fresh asparagus. Reduce heat to medium. Cover and cook 5 to 8 minutes or until crisp-tender. Drain.

1. Preheat oven to 350°F. Grease 13×9-inch casserole; set aside.

2. Heat oil in small skillet over medium heat. Add bell peppers, onion and garlic; cook and stir until crisp-tender.

3. Mix soup, eggs, ricotta cheese and 1 cup Cheddar cheese in large bowl until well blended. Add onion mixture, chicken, asparagus and noodles; mix well. Season with pepper, if desired.

4. Spread mixture evenly in prepared casserole. Top with remaining 1 cup Cheddar cheese.

5. Bake 30 minutes or until center is set and cheese is bubbly. Let stand 5 minutes before serving. Garnish as desired. *Makes 12 servings*

Quickest Chicken Cacciatore

4 BUTTERBALL® Boneless Skinless Chicken Thighs
2 tablespoons butter or margarine
1 jar (14 ounces) chunky-style meatless spaghetti sauce
1 jar (2½ ounces) sliced mushrooms, drained
½ cup chopped green bell pepper
¼ cup dry red wine
1 package (9 ounces) refrigerated fettuccine, cooked and drained

Cut each thigh lengthwise into 3 pieces. Melt butter in large skillet over medium heat. Add chicken; cook 8 to 10 minutes or until no longer pink in center. Add remaining ingredients except fettuccine. Cook and stir until heated through. Serve over fettuccine. *Makes 4 servings*

Prep Time: 15 minutes

Chicken-Asparagus Casserole

Noodles Thai Style

- ¼ cup ketchup
- 2 tablespoons reduced-sodium soy sauce
- 1 tablespoon sugar
- ¼ to ½ teaspoon crushed red pepper
- ¼ teaspoon ground ginger
- 2 teaspoons FLEISCHMANN'S® Original Spread (70% Corn Oil), divided
- 1 cup EGG BEATERS® Healthy Real Egg Substitute
- 8 green onions, cut in 1½-inch pieces
- 1 clove garlic, minced
- ¾ pound fresh bean sprouts, rinsed and well drained
- 8 ounces linguine, cooked and drained
- ¼ cup PLANTERS® Dry Roasted Unsalted Peanuts, chopped

In small bowl, combine ketchup, soy sauce, sugar, pepper and ginger; set aside.

In large nonstick skillet, over medium heat, melt 1 teaspoon spread. Pour Egg Beaters® into skillet. Cook, stirring occasionally until set. Remove to another small bowl.

In same skillet, over medium heat, sauté green onions and garlic in remaining spread for 2 minutes. Stir in bean sprouts; cook for 2 minutes. Stir in ketchup mixture. Cook until heated through. Transfer to large bowl; add eggs and linguine. Toss until combined. Top with peanuts.

Makes 6 (1-cup) servings

Prep Time: 25 minutes
Cook Time: 5 minutes

Chicken Paprika

- 3 tablespoons all-purpose flour
- 1 tablespoon paprika
- ¼ teaspoon salt
- ⅛ teaspoon black pepper
- 4 chicken breasts, skinned (about 1½ pounds)
- 1 teaspoon olive oil
- 1 medium onion, chopped
- 1 cup chicken broth
- ¼ cup sour cream
  Hot cooked spaetzel or noodles

Combine flour, paprika, salt and pepper on sheet of waxed paper. Coat chicken breasts with flour mixture. Reserve remaining flour mixture.

Heat oil in large skillet over medium heat. Add chicken; cook about 10 minutes or until browned on all sides. Remove chicken from skillet.

Add onion to same skillet; cook 2 minutes. Stir in remaining flour mixture. Gradually stir in chicken broth; cook and stir until mixture comes to a boil. Return chicken to skillet. Reduce heat to low; cover and simmer 25 minutes or until juices run clear.

Remove chicken to platter. Spoon off fat from gravy in skillet. Add sour cream to skillet; stir to combine. Serve with spaetzel. Garnish with fresh parsley, if desired. *Makes 4 servings*

Lightened Up

Turkey Vegetable Chili Mac

Nonstick cooking spray
¾ pound ground turkey breast
½ cup chopped onion
2 cloves garlic, minced
1 can (about 15 ounces) black beans, rinsed and drained
1 can (14½ ounces) Mexican-style stewed tomatoes, undrained

1 can (14½ ounces) no-salt-added diced tomatoes, undrained
1 cup frozen whole kernel corn
1 teaspoon Mexican seasoning
½ cup uncooked elbow macaroni
⅓ cup reduced-fat sour cream

1. Spray large nonstick saucepan or Dutch oven with cooking spray; heat over medium heat until hot. Add turkey, onion and garlic; cook 5 minutes or until turkey is no longer pink, stirring to crumble.

2. Stir beans, tomatoes with liquid, corn and Mexican seasoning into saucepan; bring to a boil over high heat. Cover; reduce heat to low. Simmer 15 minutes, stirring occasionally.

3. Meanwhile, cook pasta according to package directions, omitting salt. Rinse; drain. Stir into saucepan. Simmer, uncovered, 2 to 3 minutes or until heated through.

4. Top each serving with dollop of sour cream. *Makes 6 servings*

Nutrients per Serving: Calories 236, Total Fat 6 g, Cholesterol 25 mg, Sodium 445 mg

Creamy Pasta Primavera

1 bag (16 ounces) BIRDS EYE® frozen Pasta Secrets Primavera
½ cup 1% milk
2 packages (3 ounces each) cream cheese, cubed
1 cup cubed ham
¼ cup grated Parmesan cheese

● In large skillet, heat Pasta Secrets in milk over medium heat to a simmer; cover and simmer 7 to 9 minutes or until vegetables are tender.

● Add cream cheese; reduce heat to low and cook until cream cheese is melted, stirring often.

● Stir in ham and cheese; cover and cook 5 minutes more.

Makes 4 servings

Broccoli and Beef Pasta

1 pound lean ground beef
2 cloves garlic, minced
1 can (14½ ounces) beef broth
1 medium onion, thinly sliced
1 cup uncooked rotini pasta
½ teaspoon dried basil leaves
½ teaspoon dried oregano leaves
½ teaspoon dried thyme leaves
1 can Italian-style tomatoes, undrained
2 cups broccoli florets *or* 1 package (10 ounces) frozen broccoli, thawed
3 ounces shredded Cheddar cheese or grated Parmesan cheese

1. Combine meat and garlic in large nonstick skillet; cook over high heat until meat is no longer pink, breaking meat apart with wooden spoon. Pour off drippings. Place meat in large bowl; set aside.

2. Add broth, onion, pasta, basil, oregano and thyme to skillet. Bring to a boil. Reduce heat to medium-high and boil 10 minutes (if using frozen broccoli, boil 15 minutes); add tomatoes and their juice. Increase heat to high and bring to a boil; stir in broccoli. Cook, uncovered, 6 to 8 minutes, stirring occasionally, until broccoli is crisp-tender and pasta is tender. Return meat to skillet and stir 3 to 4 minutes or until heated through.

3. With slotted spoon, transfer to serving platter. Sprinkle with cheese. Cover with lid or tent with foil several minutes, until cheese melts. Meanwhile, bring juice left in skillet to a boil over high heat. Boil until thick and reduced to 3 to 4 tablespoons. Spoon over meat.

Makes 4 servings

Serving Suggestion: Serve with garlic bread.

Prep and Cook Time: 30 minutes

Sausage Bake

1 cup uncooked egg noodles
1 bag (16 ounces) BIRDS EYE® frozen Cut Green Beans
1 pound smoked sausage links, fully cooked
1 can (15 ounces) cream of celery soup
½ teaspoon *each* sage, celery salt and garlic powder

● In large saucepan, cook noodles according to package directions. Add green beans during last 10 minutes; drain and return to pan.

● Meanwhile, cut sausage into ½-inch pieces.

● Add all ingredients to noodles and beans; toss together.

● Cook over medium heat 3 to 5 minutes or until heated through. Add salt and pepper to taste.

Makes 4 servings

Prep Time: 2 minutes
Cook Time: 15 minutes

Broccoli and Beef Pasta

Spicy Tuna and Linguine with Garlic and Pine Nuts

2 tablespoons olive oil
4 cloves garlic, minced
2 cups sliced mushrooms
½ cup chopped onion
½ teaspoon crushed red pepper
2½ cups chopped plum tomatoes
1 can (14½ ounces) chicken broth plus water to equal 2 cups
½ teaspoon salt
¼ teaspoon coarsely ground black pepper
1 package (9 ounces) uncooked fresh linguine
1 can (12 ounces) STARKIST® Solid White Tuna, drained and chunked
⅓ cup chopped fresh cilantro
⅓ cup toasted pine nuts or almonds

In 12-inch skillet, heat olive oil over medium-high heat; sauté garlic, mushrooms, onion and red pepper until golden brown. Add tomatoes, chicken broth mixture, salt and black pepper; bring to a boil.

Separate uncooked linguine into strands; place in skillet and spoon sauce over. Reduce heat to simmer; cook, covered, 4 more minutes or until cooked through. Toss gently; add tuna and cilantro and toss again. Sprinkle with pine nuts.

Makes 4 to 6 servings

Veggie Tuna Pasta

1 package (16 ounces) medium pasta shells
1 bag (16 ounces) BIRDS EYE® frozen Farm Fresh Mixtures Broccoli, Corn & Red Peppers
1 can (10 ounces) chunky light tuna, packed in water
1 can (10¾ ounces) reduced-fat cream of mushroom soup

● In large saucepan, cook pasta according to package directions. Add vegetables during last 10 minutes; drain and return to saucepan.

● Stir in tuna and soup. Add salt and pepper to taste. Cook over medium heat until heated through.

Makes 4 servings

Variation: Stir in 1 can (4 to 6 ounces) chopped ripe olives with tuna.

To toast nuts, place in an ungreased skillet and cook over medium heat, stirring often, until golden.

Spicy Tuna and Linguine with Garlic and Pine Nuts

Skillet Shrimp with Rotelle

3 tablespoons FILIPPO BERIO® Olive Oil
1 medium onion, chopped
2 cloves garlic, minced
2 cups uncooked rotelle or other curly pasta
3 cups chicken broth
1 cup asparagus tips
¾ pound raw medium shrimp, shelled and deveined
¾ cup halved cherry tomatoes
¼ cup pitted ripe olives
1 teaspoon dried oregano leaves
1 teaspoon dried basil leaves
Salt and freshly ground black pepper

In large skillet, heat olive oil over medium heat until hot. Add onion and garlic; cook and stir 4 to 6 minutes or until onion is softened, but not brown. Add pasta; stir to coat pasta with oil. Increase heat to high; pour in chicken broth. Bring to a boil. Reduce heat to medium-high; cook, stirring occasionally, 12 to 14 minutes or until pasta is al dente (tender but still firm). Add asparagus. Cook, stirring frequently, 2 to 3 minutes or until asparagus is tender-crisp. Add shrimp, tomatoes, olives, oregano and basil. Cook, stirring frequently, 3 minutes or until liquid is almost completely absorbed and shrimp are opaque (do not overcook shrimp). Season to taste with salt and pepper.

Makes 4 to 6 servings

Fettucine à la Tuna

½ cup broccoli florets
½ cup chopped red bell pepper
1 tablespoon sliced green onion
1 clove garlic, minced
1 tablespoon butter or margarine
¼ cup low-fat milk
¼ cup low-fat ricotta cheese
Salt and pepper to taste
1 can (6 ounces) STARKIST® Tuna, drained and broken into small chunks
2 ounces fettucine or linguine, cooked and drained
1 tablespoon grated Parmesan or Romano cheese (optional)

In small saucepan, steam broccoli and bell pepper over simmering water 5 minutes. Drain liquid from vegetables and remove steamer. In same pan sauté onion and garlic in butter 2 minutes. Add milk and ricotta cheese, stirring well with wire whisk. Season to taste with salt and pepper. Add tuna and vegetables; cook over low heat 2 minutes. Toss fettucine with tuna mixture. Spoon onto plate; sprinkle with Parmesan cheese, if desired.

Makes 1 serving

Prep Time: 15 minutes

Skillet Shrimp with Rotelle

Greek Lamb Braised with Vegetables

¼ cup FILIPPO BERIO® Olive Oil
2½ pounds lean boneless lamb, cut into 1½-inch cubes
1 cup chicken broth
½ cup dry white wine
2 medium carrots, diagonally cut into 1-inch pieces
2 ribs celery, diagonally cut into 1-inch pieces
½ medium bulb fennel, cut into ¼-inch-thick slices lengthwise through stem
1 (14-ounce) can artichoke hearts, drained and cut into quarters lengthwise
3 green onions, trimmed and cut into 1½-inch pieces
  Salt and freshly ground black pepper
8 ounces uncooked orzo pasta
  Chopped fresh parsley

In Dutch oven, heat olive oil over medium-high heat until hot. Add lamb; cook and stir 5 minutes or until lightly browned. Add broth and wine; cover. Bring mixture to a boil. Reduce heat to low, simmer 1½ hours. Add carrots, celery, fennel, artichokes and green onions. Simmer 15 to 20 minutes or until lamb and vegetables are tender.

Season to taste with salt and pepper. Meanwhile, cook orzo according to package directions until al dente (tender but still firm). Drain. Serve lamb mixture over orzo. Top with parsley.

Makes 6 servings

Elaine's Tuna Tetrazzini

8 ounces fresh mushrooms, sliced
1 cup chopped onion
2 tablespoons vegetable oil
3 tablespoons all-purpose flour
1 cup chicken broth
½ cup low-fat milk
½ teaspoon paprika
½ teaspoon salt
¼ teaspoon pepper
1 can (6 ounces) STARKIST® Tuna, drained and broken into chunks
¼ cup grated Parmesan or Romano cheese
2 tablespoons minced parsley
8 ounces thin spaghetti or linguine, broken into halves, hot cooked

In large skillet, sauté mushrooms and onion in oil for 3 minutes, or until limp. Sprinkle flour over vegetables; stir until blended. Add chicken broth and milk all at once; cook and stir until mixture thickens and bubbles. Stir in paprika, salt and pepper; cook 2 minutes more. Stir in tuna, cheese and parsley; cook 1 to 2 minutes, or until heated through. Spoon over pasta.   *Makes 4 servings*

Prep Time: 20 minutes

Country Classic

Chicken Carbonara

1 pound chicken tenders
1 jar (12 ounces) Alfredo sauce
1 cup milk
1⅓ cups FRENCH'S® French Fried
    Onions, divided

½ of a 10-ounce package frozen
    peas, thawed and drained
2 tablespoons real bacon bits*
Hot cooked pasta

*Or, substitute 2 strips crumbled, cooked bacon for real bacon bits.

Spray large nonstick skillet with nonstick cooking spray; heat over high heat.
Add chicken; cook and stir about 5 minutes or until browned.

Stir in Alfredo sauce and milk. Add ⅔ *cup* French Fried Onions, peas and
bacon bits. Bring to a boil. Reduce heat to low. Cook 5 minutes, stirring
occasionally. Serve over pasta. Sprinkle with remaining ⅔ *cup* onions.

Makes 4 to 6 servings

Prep Time: 10 minutes
Cook Time: 10 minutes

Zesty Garlic Chicken

¾ pound boneless, skinless chicken
    breast, cut into 1-inch cubes
1 tablespoon vegetable oil
3 tablespoons lime or lemon juice
2 teaspoons Worcestershire sauce
2 teaspoons soy sauce
1 bag (16 ounces) BIRDS EYE® frozen
    Pasta Secrets Zesty Garlic

● In large skillet, cook and stir chicken
in oil over medium heat until no longer
pink in center.

● Stir in lime juice, Worcestershire and
soy sauce.

● Add Pasta Secrets; stir well.

● Cover and cook 7 to 9 minutes or
until vegetables are crisp-tender, stirring
occasionally. *Makes 4 servings*

Prep Time: 5 minutes
Cook Time: 20 minutes

Smoked Sausage and Noodle Skillet

1 tablespoon vegetable oil
1 pound HILLSHIRE FARM® Smoked Sausage, cut into ¼-inch slices
1 onion, chopped
3 cups frozen broccoli, cauliflower and carrots mixture
4 ounces uncooked medium-size noodles or curly noodles
1 can (10¾ ounces) reduced-sodium condensed cream of celery soup, undiluted
1 cup reduced-sodium chicken broth
½ teaspoon dried marjoram leaves
¼ teaspoon black pepper

Heat oil in medium skillet over medium heat. Cook and stir Smoked Sausage and onion 3 to 4 minutes. Stir in frozen vegetables, noodles, soup, chicken broth, ¾ cup water, marjoram and pepper. Bring to a boil; reduce heat. Simmer, covered, 12 to 15 minutes or until noodles are tender, stirring occasionally.   *Makes 4 servings*

Store onions in a cool, dry place away from other foods that will absorb their odor.

Thai Peanut Noodle Stir-Fry

1 cup COLLEGE INN® Chicken Broth or Lower Sodium Chicken Broth
½ cup GREY POUPON® Dijon Mustard
⅓ cup creamy peanut butter
3 tablespoons firmly packed light brown sugar
2 tablespoons soy sauce
1 clove garlic, crushed
½ teaspoon minced fresh ginger
1 tablespoon cornstarch
4 cups cut-up vegetables (red pepper, carrot, mushrooms, green onions, pea pods)
1 tablespoon vegetable oil
1 pound linguine, cooked
  Chopped peanuts and scallion brushes for garnish

In medium saucepan, combine chicken broth, mustard, peanut butter, sugar, soy sauce, garlic, ginger and cornstarch. Cook over medium heat until mixture thickens and begins to boil; reduce heat and keep warm.

In large skillet, over medium-high heat, sauté vegetables in oil until tender, about 5 minutes. In large serving bowl, combine hot cooked pasta, vegetables and peanut sauce, tossing until well coated. Garnish with chopped peanuts and scallion brushes. Serve immediately.   *Makes 4 to 6 servings*

Smoked Sausage and Noodle Skillet

Beef "Chow Fun" Stir-Fry

½ **pound boneless tender beef steak (sirloin, rib eye or top loin)**
7 **tablespoons KIKKOMAN® Stir-Fry Sauce, divided**
6 **ounces uncooked extra wide egg noodles**
6 **tablespoons beef broth**
¼ **teaspoon white pepper**
2 **tablespoons vegetable oil, divided**
1 **clove garlic, minced**
1 **teaspoon minced fresh ginger root**
1 **onion, chunked**
1 **pound romaine lettuce, washed and cut crosswise into 1-inch strips**

Cut beef across grain into thin slices 1 inch wide; coat with 1 tablespoon stir-fry sauce. Let stand 30 minutes. Meanwhile, cook noodles according to package directions in lightly salted water; drain. Combine remaining 6 tablespoons stir-fry sauce, beef broth and pepper in small bowl; set aside. Heat 1 tablespoon oil in hot wok or large skillet. Add beef and stir-fry 1 minute; remove. Heat remaining 1 tablespoon oil in same pan. Add garlic and ginger; stir-fry 10 seconds, or until fragrant. Add onion; stir-fry 2 minutes. Add romaine; stir-fry 2 minutes longer. Reduce heat to medium. Add noodles and stir-fry sauce mixture; cook and stir until noodles are thoroughly heated, about 2 minutes. Stir in beef; heat through. Serve immediately.

Makes 4 servings

Soba Stir-Fry

8 **ounces uncooked soba noodles (Japanese buckwheat pasta)**
1 **tablespoon light olive oil**
2 **cups sliced fresh shiitake mushrooms**
1 **medium red bell pepper, cut into thin strips**
2 **whole dried red peppers *or* ¼ teaspoon red pepper flakes**
1 **clove garlic, minced**
2 **cups shredded napa cabbage**
½ **cup ⅓-less-salt chicken broth**
2 **tablespoons reduced-sodium tamari or soy sauce**
1 **tablespoon rice wine or dry sherry**
2 **teaspoons cornstarch**
1 **package (14 ounces) firm tofu, drained and cut into 1-inch cubes**
2 **green onions, thinly sliced**

1. Cook noodles according to package directions, omitting salt. Drain and set aside.

2. Heat oil in large nonstick skillet or wok over medium heat. Add mushrooms, bell pepper, dried peppers and garlic. Cook 3 minutes or until mushrooms are tender.

3. Add cabbage. Cover. Cook 2 minutes or until cabbage is wilted.

4. Combine chicken broth, tamari, rice wine and cornstarch in small bowl. Stir sauce into vegetable mixture. Cook 2 minutes or until sauce is bubbly.

5. Stir in tofu and noodles; toss gently until heated through. Sprinkle with green onions. Serve immediately.

Makes 4 (2-cup) servings

Beef "Chow Fun" Stir-Fry

Stir-Fry Chicken & Sesame Noodle Salad

8 ounces uncooked vermicelli
10 cherry tomatoes, cut into halves
2 carrots, cut into julienne strips
½ cup chopped green onions and tops
1 tablespoon sesame seed, toasted
5 tablespoons KIKKOMAN® Stir-Fry Sauce, divided
3 tablespoons vinegar
2 tablespoons water
1 tablespoon sugar
1 clove garlic, minced
1 teaspoon minced fresh ginger root
½ pound boneless, skinless chicken, cut into thin strips
3 tablespoons vegetable oil, divided
2 ounces fresh snow peas, trimmed and cut into julienne strips

Cook vermicelli according to package directions, omitting salt; drain. Cool under cold water; drain thoroughly. Combine vermicelli, tomatoes, carrots, green onions and sesame seed in large bowl. Blend 4 tablespoons stir-fry sauce, vinegar, water, sugar, garlic and ginger in small bowl; set aside. Coat chicken with remaining 1 tablespoon stir-fry sauce in small bowl. Heat 1 tablespoon oil in hot wok or large skillet over high heat. Add chicken and stir-fry 2 minutes; remove. Reduce heat to medium; heat remaining 2 tablespoons oil in same pan. Add snow peas; stir-fry 1 minute. Add chicken and stir-fry sauce mixture; cook and stir only until chicken and snow peas are coated with sauce and heated through. Pour over noodles and toss to coat well.

Makes 4 servings

Shrimp and Vegetables with Lo Mein Noodles

2 tablespoons vegetable oil
1 pound medium shrimp, peeled
2 packages (21 ounces each) frozen lo mein stir-fry mix with sauce
¼ cup peanuts
Fresh cilantro
1 small wedge cabbage

1. Heat oil in wok or large skillet over medium-high heat. Add shrimp; stir-fry 3 minutes or until shrimp are pink and opaque. Remove shrimp from wok to medium bowl. Set aside.

2. Remove sauce packet from stir-fry mix. Add frozen vegetables and noodles to wok; stir in sauce. Cover and cook 7 to 8 minutes, stirring frequently.

3. While vegetable mixture is cooking, chop peanuts and enough cilantro to measure 2 tablespoons. Shred cabbage.

4. Stir shrimp, peanuts and cilantro into vegetable mixture; heat through. Serve immediately with cabbage.

Makes 6 servings

Prep and Cook Time: 19 minutes

Chicken Thai Stir-Fry

2 tablespoons vegetable oil
4 broiler-fryer chicken breast halves, boned, skinned and cut into 1/2-inch strips
2 teaspoons grated fresh ginger
2 cloves garlic, minced
2 cups broccoli flowerets
1 medium yellow squash, cut into 1/4-inch slices
1 medium red bell pepper, cut into 2-inch strips
1/3 cup creamy peanut butter
1/4 cup reduced-sodium soy sauce
2 tablespoons white vinegar
2 teaspoons sugar
1/2 teaspoon crushed red pepper
1/3 cup reduced-sodium chicken broth, fat skimmed
8 ounces linguine, cooked according to package directions
2 green onions, white and green parts, thinly sliced

In large skillet, heat oil over medium-high heat. Add chicken, ginger and garlic and cook, stirring, about 5 minutes or until chicken is lightly browned and fork-tender. Remove chicken mixture to bowl; set aside. To drippings in same skillet, add broccoli, squash and red bell pepper strips. Cook, stirring, about 5 minutes or until vegetables are crisp-tender. Remove vegetables to bowl with chicken; set aside. To same skillet, add peanut butter, soy sauce, vinegar, sugar and crushed red pepper; stir in chicken broth. Return chicken and vegetables to pan; heat through. Serve over linguine. Sprinkle with green onions.

Makes 4 servings

Favorite recipe from **Delmarva Poultry Industry, Inc.**

Hot & Sour Noodle Stir-Fry

2 teaspoons cornstarch
2 teaspoons KIKKOMAN® Lite Teriyaki Marinade & Sauce
1/2 pound boneless tender beef steak (sirloin, rib eye or top loin), cut into thin strips
4 ounces uncooked fine egg noodles
1/4 cup KIKKOMAN® Lite Teriyaki Marinade & Sauce
2 tablespoons water
1 teaspoon vinegar
2 tablespoons vegetable oil, divided
1 clove garlic, minced
1/4 pound fresh snow peas, trimmed and cut into julienne strips
1 red bell pepper, cut into julienne strips
2 tablespoons minced unsalted roasted peanuts
1 tablespoon minced fresh cilantro

Combine cornstarch and 2 teaspoons lite teriyaki sauce in small bowl; stir in beef. Let stand 30 minutes. Meanwhile, cook egg noodles according to package directions, omitting salt; drain. Combine 1/4 cup lite teriyaki sauce, water and vinegar; set aside. Heat 1 tablespoon oil in hot wok or large skillet over high heat. Add beef and garlic; stir-fry 1 minute. Remove. Heat remaining 1 tablespoon oil in same pan. Add snow peas and bell pepper; stir-fry 1 minute. Stir in noodles until thoroughly heated. Add beef and lite teriyaki sauce mixture. Cook and stir only until all pieces are coated with sauce. Remove from heat; add peanuts and cilantro, tossing to combine. Serve immediately.

Makes 4 servings

Country
Classic

Minestrone Soup

¾ cup small shell pasta
2 cans (about 14 ounces each)
vegetable broth
1 can (28 ounces) crushed
tomatoes in tomato purée
1 can (15 ounces) white beans,
drained and rinsed

1 package (16 ounces) frozen
vegetable medley, such as
broccoli, green beans,
carrots and red peppers
4 to 6 teaspoons prepared pesto

1. Bring 4 cups water to a boil in large saucepan over high heat. Stir in pasta; cook 8 to 10 minutes or until tender. Drain.

2. While pasta is cooking, combine broth, tomatoes and beans in Dutch oven. Cover and bring to a boil over high heat. Reduce heat to low; simmer 3 to 5 minutes.

3. Add vegetables to broth mixture and return to a boil over high heat. Stir in pasta. Ladle soup into bowls; spoon about 1 teaspoon pesto in center of each serving. *Makes 4 to 6 servings*

All-in-One Burger Stew

1 pound lean ground beef
2 cups frozen Italian vegetables
1 can (14½ ounces) chopped
tomatoes with basil and garlic
1 can (about 14 ounces) beef broth
2½ cups uncooked medium egg
noodles

1. Cook meat in Dutch oven or large skillet over medium-high heat until no longer pink, breaking meat apart with wooden spoon. Drain drippings.

2. Add vegetables, tomatoes and broth; bring to a boil over high heat.

3. Add noodles; reduce heat to medium. Cover and cook 12 to 15 minutes or until noodles have absorbed liquid and vegetables are tender. Add salt and pepper to taste.

Makes 6 servings

Prep and Cook Time: 25 minutes

All-in-One Burger Stew

Lightened Up

Tomato and Turkey Soup with Pesto

1 cup uncooked rotini pasta
1 can (10¾ ounces) reduced-
    sodium tomato soup
1 cup fat-free (skim) milk
2 cups (8 ounces) frozen Italian-
    style vegetables

2 tablespoons prepared pesto
1 cup coarsely chopped skinless
    cooked turkey
2 tablespoons grated Parmesan
    cheese

1. Cook pasta according to package directions, omitting salt. Drain and rinse well under cold water until pasta is cool; drain well.

2. Meanwhile, combine soup, milk, vegetables and pesto in medium saucepan. Bring to a boil over medium heat; reduce heat to low. Simmer, covered, 10 minutes or until vegetables are tender. Add pasta and turkey. Cook 3 minutes or until heated through. Sprinkle with cheese just before serving.   *Makes 4 servings*

Nutrients per Serving: Calories 299, Total Fat 6 g, Cholesterol 40 mg, Sodium 438 mg

Pork Pasta Fazool

½ pound lean ground pork
1 small onion, diced
1 clove garlic, minced
1 can (15 ounces) cannellini beans,
    drained
1 can (14½ ounces) chicken broth
1 can (14½ ounces) Italian-style
    chopped tomatoes
½ cup small pasta shells or macaroni
1 teaspoon dried oregano leaves
½ teaspoon salt
½ teaspoon crushed fennel seed
½ teaspoon coarsely ground black
    pepper
¼ teaspoon crushed red pepper flakes

In large heavy saucepan brown and crumble ground pork. Stir in onion and garlic; cook and stir until onion is soft, about 3 minutes. Stir in remaining ingredients; bring to a boil, reduce heat and simmer 10 to 12 minutes or until pasta is tender.

Makes 6 (1-cup) servings

Prep Time: 20 minutes

Favorite recipe from **National Pork Producers Council**

Tomato and Turkey Soup with Pesto

RISE 'N' SHINE

Dixie Casserole

White Sauce (recipe follows)
1 pound HILLSHIRE FARM® Gourmet
Cooked Sausage—Chicken and
Turkey with Wild Rice and
Herbs, sliced
1 can (17 ounces) corn, drained
4 hard-cooked eggs, sliced
¾ cup soft bread crumbs
1 tablespoon butter or margarine,
melted

Preheat oven to 350°F.

Prepare White Sauce; set aside. Lightly brown Gourmet Sausage in large skillet over medium-high heat. Combine sausage, corn and eggs in large bowl; add White Sauce and stir together. Pour sausage mixture into small casserole.

Toss bread crumbs with butter in small bowl; sprinkle over top of sausage mixture. Bake, uncovered, 30 minutes or until heated through.

Makes 6 servings

White Sauce

¼ cup butter or margarine
¼ cup all-purpose flour
½ teaspoon salt
2 cups milk

Melt butter in small saucepan over medium heat; stir in flour and salt. Add milk; cook and stir until mixture is thickened and bubbly. Cook and stir 1 to 2 minutes more.

Makes about 2½ cups

Dixie Casserole

Country Classic

Quiche Lorraine Florentine

1 (10-ounce) package frozen
  chopped spinach, thawed
  and well drained
1 cup shredded Swiss cheese
  (4 ounces)
4 slices bacon, cooked and
  crumbled
2 tablespoons chopped green
  onions

1 (9-inch) unbaked pastry shell
3 eggs, slightly beaten
1 cup light cream or half-and-
  half
¼ cup GREY POUPON® Dijon
  Mustard

Combine spinach, cheese, bacon and green onions. Spoon mixture evenly into pastry shell.

In small bowl, blend eggs, cream and mustard. Pour evenly over spinach mixture. Bake at 375°F for 35 to 40 minutes or until knife inserted in center comes out clean. Let stand 10 minutes before serving. To serve, cut into wedges.

Makes 8 servings

Skillet Sausage with Potatoes and Rosemary

1 tablespoon vegetable oil
3 cups diced red skin potatoes
1 cup diced onion
1 pound BOB EVANS® Original
  Recipe Roll Sausage
½ teaspoon dried rosemary
¼ teaspoon rubbed sage
  Salt and black pepper to taste
2 tablespoons chopped fresh parsley

Heat oil in large skillet over medium-high heat 1 minute. Add potatoes; cook 5 to 10 minutes or until slightly brown, stirring occasionally. Add onion; cook until tender. Add crumbled sausage; cook until browned. Add rosemary, sage, salt and pepper; cook and stir until well blended. Transfer to serving platter and garnish with parsley. Refrigerate leftovers.

Makes 4 to 6 servings

Quiche Lorraine Florentine

Parmesan and Roasted Red Pepper Strata

1 loaf (16 ounces) French bread, cut into 1/2-inch-thick slices
2 jars (7 1/2 ounces each) roasted red peppers, drained and cut into 1/2-inch pieces
1 cup grated Parmesan cheese
1 cup sliced green onions
3 cups (12 ounces) shredded mozzarella cheese
8 eggs
3/4 cup reduced-fat (2%) milk
1 container (7 ounces) prepared pesto
2 teaspoons bottled minced garlic
3/4 teaspoon salt

1. Grease 13×9-inch baking dish. Arrange half the bread slices in single layer on bottom of prepared baking dish. Top bread with half the red peppers, 1/2 cup Parmesan, 1/2 cup green onions and 1 1/2 cups mozzarella. Repeat layers with remaining bread, red peppers, Parmesan, green onions and mozzarella.

2. Combine eggs, milk, pesto, garlic and salt in medium bowl; whisk to combine. Pour egg mixture evenly over strata. Cover and refrigerate overnight.

3. Preheat oven to 375°F. Bake, uncovered, 30 minutes or until hot and bubbly. *Makes 6 servings*

SPAM™ Hash Brown Bake

1 (32-ounce) package frozen hash brown potatoes, thawed slightly
1/2 cup butter or margarine, melted
1 teaspoon salt
1 teaspoon black pepper
1/2 teaspoon garlic powder
2 cups (8 ounces) shredded Cheddar cheese
1 (12-ounce) can SPAM® Luncheon Meat, cubed
1 (10 3/4-ounce) can cream of chicken soup
1 1/2 cups sour cream
1/2 cup milk
1/2 cup chopped onion
1 (4.25-ounce) jar CHI-CHI'S® Diced Green Chilies, drained
2 cups crushed potato chips

Heat oven to 350°F. In large bowl, combine potatoes, melted butter, salt, pepper and garlic powder. In separate large bowl, combine cheese, SPAM®, soup, sour cream, milk, onion and green chilies. Add SPAM™ mixture to potato mixture; mix well. Pour into 2-quart baking dish. Sprinkle with potato chips. Bake 45 to 60 minutes or until thoroughly heated.

Makes 8 servings

Parmesan and Roasted Red Pepper Strata

Egg & Sausage Casserole

½ pound pork sausage
3 tablespoons margarine or butter, divided
2 tablespoons all-purpose flour
¼ teaspoon salt
¼ teaspoon black pepper
1¼ cups milk
2 cups frozen hash brown potatoes
4 eggs, hard-boiled and sliced
½ cup cornflake crumbs
¼ cup sliced green onions

Preheat oven to 350°F. Spray 2-quart oval baking dish with nonstick cooking spray.

Crumble sausage into large skillet; brown over medium-high heat until no longer pink, stirring to separate meat. Drain sausage on paper towels. Discard fat and wipe skillet with paper towel.

Melt 2 tablespoons margarine in same skillet over medium heat. Stir in flour, salt and pepper until smooth. Gradually stir in milk; cook and stir until thickened. Add sausage, potatoes and eggs; stir to combine. Pour into prepared dish.

Melt remaining 1 tablespoon margarine. Combine cornflake crumbs and melted margarine in small bowl; sprinkle evenly over casserole.

Bake, uncovered, 30 minutes or until hot and bubbly. Sprinkle with onions.
Makes 6 servings

Spinach & Egg Casserole

1 box (10 ounces) BIRDS EYE® frozen Chopped Spinach
1 can (15 ounces) Cheddar cheese soup
1 tablespoon mustard
½ pound deli ham, cut into ¼-inch cubes
4 hard-boiled eggs, chopped or sliced

●Preheat oven to 350°F.

●In large saucepan, cook spinach according to package directions; drain well.

●Stir in soup, mustard and ham.

●Pour into 9×9-inch baking pan. Top with eggs.

●Bake 15 to 20 minutes or until heated through. *Makes 4 servings*

Prep Time: 10 minutes
Cook Time: 15 to 20 minutes

Eggs cooked a day ahead will be much easier to peel.

Lightened Up

Farmstand Frittata

½ cup chopped onion
1 medium red bell pepper,
    seeded, cut into thin strips
1 cup broccoli flowerets,
    blanched, drained
1 cup cooked, quartered,
    unpeeled red-skinned
    potatoes

6 egg whites
1 cup cholesterol-free egg
    substitute
1 tablespoon chopped parsley
½ teaspoon salt
¼ teaspoon ground black pepper
½ cup (2 ounces) shredded
    reduced-fat Cheddar cheese

1. Spray large nonstick ovenproof skillet with nonstick cooking spray; heat over medium heat until hot. Add onion and bell pepper; cook and stir until crisp-tender. Add broccoli and potatoes; cook and stir until heated through.

2. Whisk together egg whites, egg substitute, parsley, salt and black pepper in medium bowl.

3. Spread vegetables into even layer in skillet. Pour egg white mixture over vegetables; cover and cook over medium heat 10 to 12 minutes or until egg mixture is set. Meanwhile, preheat broiler. Top fritatta with cheese. Broil 4 inches from heat 1 minute or until cheese is golden brown. Cut into wedges.

Makes 4 servings

Nutrients per Serving: Calories 179, Total Fat 3 g, Cholesterol 10 mg, Sodium 574 mg

Lit'l Links Soufflé

8 slices white bread
2 cups (8 ounces) shredded Cheddar
    cheese
1 pound HILLSHIRE FARM® Lit'l
    Polskas
6 eggs
2¾ cups milk
¾ teaspoon dry mustard

Spread bread in bottom of greased 13×9-inch baking pan. Sprinkle cheese over top of bread. Arrange Lit'l Polskas on top of cheese. Beat eggs with milk and mustard in large bowl; pour over links. Cover pan with aluminum foil; refrigerate overnight. Preheat oven to 300°F. Bake egg mixture 1½ hours or until puffy and brown.

Makes 4 to 6 servings

Ham and Cheese Frittata

1 tablespoon vegetable oil
1 cup chopped red onion
½ cup chopped green bell pepper
1 teaspoon minced garlic
1 cup (6 ounces) slivered ALPINE LACE® Boneless Cooked Ham
1 cup egg substitute *or* 4 large eggs
3 large egg whites
1 cup (4 ounces) shredded ALPINE LACE® Reduced Fat Cheddar Cheese, divided
¼ cup whole fresh tarragon leaves *or* 2 teaspoons dried tarragon
½ teaspoon salt
¼ teaspoon cracked black pepper
2 large plum tomatoes, thinly sliced

1. Preheat the broiler. In a large broilerproof skillet, heat the oil over medium-high heat. Add the onion, bell pepper and garlic and sauté for 5 minutes or until soft. Stir in the ham and cook 3 minutes more.

2. In a medium-size bowl, whisk the egg substitute (or the 4 whole eggs) with the egg whites until foamy; fold in ½ cup of the cheese, the tarragon, salt and black pepper. Pour over the vegetable-ham mixture.

3. Reduce the heat and cook, uncovered, for 6 minutes or just until the egg mixture is set around the edges. Arrange the tomato slices on top of the frittata, in a circle around the edge and in a cluster in the center. Sprinkle with the remaining ½ cup of cheese.

4. Slide the skillet under the broiler for 1 minute or until the frittata is set in the center. Serve immediately right from the skillet! *Makes 4 servings*

South-of-the-Border Quiche Squares

1 pound BOB EVANS® Zesty Hot Roll Sausage
1 (8-ounce) package refrigerated crescent dinner roll dough
1 cup (4 ounces) shredded Monterey Jack cheese, divided
1 cup (4 ounces) shredded Cheddar cheese, divided
½ cup diced green chiles
½ cup chopped green onions
1 cup diced fresh or drained canned tomatoes
8 eggs, beaten
1 cup half-and-half
1 cup milk
2 tablespoons Dijon mustard
1 tablespoon chopped fresh parsley
½ teaspoon chili powder

Preheat oven to 350°F. Crumble and cook sausage in medium skillet over medium heat until browned. Drain well on paper towels. Unroll dough and press perforations together. Press dough on bottom and 1 inch up sides of greased 13×9×2-inch baking pan. Bake 8 minutes or until light golden. Remove from oven; sprinkle with half of cheeses. Top with chiles, onions, tomatoes, sausage and remaining cheeses. Blend eggs, half-and-half, milk, mustard, parsley and chili powder in medium bowl. Pour mixture evenly over cheese layer. Bake 25 to 30 minutes or until set. Cool 5 minutes before cutting into 8 (4-inch) squares. Serve hot. Refrigerate leftovers.

Makes 8 servings

Ham and Cheese Frittata

Summer Sausage 'n' Egg Wedges

4 eggs, beaten
1/3 cup milk
1/4 cup all-purpose flour
1/2 teaspoon baking powder
1/8 teaspoon garlic powder
2 1/2 cups (10 ounces) shredded
    Cheddar or mozzarella cheese,
    divided
1 1/2 cups diced HILLSHIRE FARM®
    Summer Sausage
1 cup cream-style cottage cheese
    with chives

Preheat oven to 375°F. Combine eggs, milk, flour, baking powder and garlic powder in medium bowl; beat until combined. Stir in 2 cups Cheddar cheese, Summer Sausage and cottage cheese. Pour into greased 9-inch pie plate. Bake, uncovered, 25 to 30 minutes or until golden and knife inserted into center comes out clean. To serve, cut into 6 wedges. Sprinkle wedges with remaining 1/2 cup Cheddar cheese. *Makes 6 servings*

Scalloped Eggs and Bacon

2 tablespoons butter or margarine
1/4 cup chopped onion
2 tablespoons all-purpose flour
1 1/2 cups milk
1/2 cup (2 ounces) shredded American
    cheese
1/2 cup (2 ounces) shredded Swiss
    cheese
6 hard-cooked eggs, sliced
10 to 12 slices HILLSHIRE FARM®
    Bacon, crisp-cooked and
    crumbled
1 1/2 cups packaged fried onions

Preheat oven to 350°F.

Melt butter in medium skillet over medium heat. Add chopped onion; sauté until tender. Whisk in flour until thoroughly combined. Add milk; continue stirring until thick. Add cheeses; stir until melted. Place 1/2 of eggs in bottom of small baking dish; pour 1/2 of cheese mixture over eggs. Sprinkle with 1/2 of Bacon and 1/2 of fried onions. Repeat layers. Bake, uncovered, 15 to 20 minutes or until heated through. *Makes 6 servings*

Kitchen Snippets

A wire cheese slicer works well to cut hard-cooked eggs if you don't have an egg slicer.

Summer Sausage 'n' Egg Wedge

Country Classic

Sausage Scramble

1 (12-ounce) package BOB
EVANS® Original Links
¼ cup chopped onion
1 tablespoon butter or
margarine
1 medium tomato, seeded and
coarsely chopped
½ cup (2 ounces) diced
processed American cheese
2 tablespoons chopped fresh
parsley

2 to 3 drops hot pepper sauce
(optional)
¼ teaspoon salt
⅛ teaspoon black pepper
8 eggs
1 tablespoon water
Buttered toast or toasted
English muffins

Cook sausage in medium skillet until browned; drain off any drippings. Cut each link into 6 or 7 pieces and set aside. Cook onion in butter in medium nonstick skillet over medium heat until tender. Add tomato; cook 2 to 3 minutes. Add cheese, parsley, hot pepper sauce, salt and black pepper; remove skillet from heat and stir to melt cheese. Beat eggs and water lightly in medium bowl. Whisk small amount of warm cheese mixture into egg mixture, then add egg mixture back into skillet. Stir in sausage; cook until eggs are scrambled but still moist. Serve over toast or English muffins. Refrigerate leftovers.

Makes 6 servings

Asparagus Frittata Casserole

3 large eggs
1½ cups 1% milk
1 teaspoon salt
1 box (10 ounces) BIRDS EYE® frozen
Deluxe Asparagus Spears,
thawed
½ cup shredded Monterey Jack or
Cheddar cheese

● Preheat oven to 400°F.

● In medium bowl, beat eggs. Add milk and salt; blend well.

● Pour mixture into greased 9×9-inch baking pan; top with asparagus.

● Sprinkle with cheese.

● Bake 15 minutes or until egg mixture is set. *Makes 4 servings*

Prep Time: 5 to 7 minutes
Cook Time: 15 minutes

Greek Spinach and Feta Pie

- 1/3 cup butter, melted
- 2 eggs
- 1 package (10 ounces) frozen chopped spinach, thawed and squeezed dry
- 1 container (15 ounces) ricotta cheese
- 1 package (4 ounces) crumbled feta cheese
- 3/4 teaspoon finely grated lemon peel
- 1/4 teaspoon black pepper
- 1/8 teaspoon ground nutmeg
- 1 package (16 ounces) frozen phyllo dough, thawed

Preheat oven to 350°F. Brush 13×9-inch baking dish lightly with butter.

Beat eggs in medium bowl. Stir in spinach, ricotta, feta, lemon peel, pepper and nutmeg. Set aside.

Cut 8 sheets of phyllo dough in half crosswise forming 16 rectangles. Cover with damp cloth to keep moist. Reserve remaining dough for another use.

Place 1 piece of dough in prepared dish; brush top lightly with butter. Top with another piece of dough and brush lightly with butter. Continue layering with 6 pieces of dough, brushing each lightly with butter. Spoon spinach mixture evenly over dough.

Top spinach mixture with piece of dough; brush lightly with butter. Repeat layering with remaining 7 pieces of dough, brushing each piece lightly with butter. Bake, uncovered, 35 to 40 minutes or until golden brown.

Makes 6 servings

Spinach and Cheese Brunch Squares

- 1 box (11 ounces) pie crust mix
- 1/3 cup cold water
- 1 package (10 ounces) frozen chopped spinach, thawed and well drained
- 1 1/3 cups FRENCH'S® French Fried Onions
- 1 cup (4 ounces) shredded Swiss cheese
- 1 container (8 ounces) low-fat sour cream
- 5 eggs
- 1 cup milk
- 1 tablespoon FRENCH'S® Deli Brown Mustard
- 1/2 teaspoon salt
- 1/8 teaspoon ground black pepper

Preheat oven to 450°F. Line 13×9×2-inch baking pan with foil; spray with nonstick cooking spray. Combine pie crust mix and water in large bowl until moistened and crumbly. Using floured bottom of measuring cup, press mixture firmly into bottom of prepared pan. Prick with fork. Bake 20 minutes or until golden. *Reduce oven temperature to 350°F.*

Layer spinach, French Fried Onions and cheese over crust. Combine sour cream, eggs, milk, mustard, salt and pepper in medium bowl; mix until well blended. Pour over vegetable and cheese layers. Bake 30 minutes or until knife inserted in center comes out clean. Let stand 10 minutes. Cut into squares* to serve.

Makes 8 main-course servings

Prep Time: 20 minutes
Cook Time: 50 minutes
Stand Time: 10 minutes

Pizza for Breakfast

1 (6½-ounce) package pizza crust
    mix
1 pound BOB EVANS® Original
    Recipe Roll Sausage
1 cup diced fresh or drained canned
    tomatoes
8 ounces fresh mushrooms, sliced
1½ cups (6 ounces) shredded
    mozzarella cheese, divided
1½ cups (6 ounces) shredded sharp
    Cheddar cheese, divided
4 eggs
    Salt and pepper to taste
    Salsa (optional)

Preheat oven to 350°F. Prepare crust
mix according to package directions.
Spread pizza dough into greased 13×9-
inch baking dish, making sure dough
evenly covers bottom and 2 inches up
sides of dish. Crumble and cook
sausage in medium skillet until
browned; drain well on paper towels.
Top crust with sausage, tomatoes,
mushrooms, 1 cup mozzarella cheese
and 1 cup Cheddar cheese. Bake 8 to
10 minutes or until crust is golden
brown at edges. Remove from oven.
Whisk eggs, salt and pepper in small
bowl; pour over pizza. Return to oven;
bake 7 to 9 minutes more or until eggs
are set. Immediately sprinkle with
remaining cheeses. Serve hot with salsa,
if desired. Refrigerate leftovers.

Makes 8 to 10 servings

Note: Refrigerated crescent roll dough
may be used instead of pizza crust mix.
Seal edges together and stretch to fit
baking dish.

Hearty Breakfast Custard Casserole

1 pound (2 medium-large) Colorado
    baking potatoes
    Salt and pepper
8 ounces low-fat bulk pork sausage,
    cooked and crumbled *or*
    6 ounces finely diced lean ham
    or 6 ounces turkey bacon,
    cooked and crumbled
⅓ cup julienne-sliced roasted red
    pepper *or* 1 jar (2 ounces) sliced
    pimientos, drained
3 eggs
1 cup low-fat milk
3 tablespoons chopped fresh chives
    or green onion tops *or*
    ¾ teaspoon dried thyme or
    oregano leaves
    Salsa and low-fat sour cream or
    plain yogurt (optional)

Heat oven to 375°F. Grease 8- or 9-inch
square baking dish or other small
casserole. Peel potatoes and slice very
thin; arrange half of the potatoes in
baking dish. Sprinkle with salt and
pepper. Cover with half of the sausage.
Arrange remaining potatoes on top;
sprinkle with salt and pepper. Top with
remaining sausage and red pepper. Beat
eggs, milk and chives until blended.
Pour over potatoes. Cover baking dish
with foil and bake 35 to 45 minutes or
until potatoes are tender. Uncover and
bake 5 to 10 minutes more. Serve with
salsa and sour cream, if desired.

Makes 4 to 5 servings

Favorite recipe from **Colorado Potato
Administrative Committee**

Pizza for Breakfast

Cheesy Country SPAM™ Puff

6 slices white bread, torn into small pieces
1¼ cups milk
3 eggs
1 tablespoon spicy mustard
½ teaspoon garlic powder
½ teaspoon paprika
1 (12-ounce) can SPAM® Luncheon Meat, cubed
2 cups (8 ounces) shredded sharp Cheddar cheese, divided
½ cup chopped onion
½ cup (2 ounces) shredded Monterey Jack cheese

Heat oven to 375°F. In large bowl, combine bread, milk, eggs, mustard, garlic powder and paprika. Beat at medium speed of electric mixer 1 minute or until smooth. Stir in SPAM®, 1 cup Cheddar cheese and onion. Pour into greased 12×8-inch baking dish. Bake 25 minutes. Top with remaining 1 cup Cheddar cheese and Monterey Jack cheese. Bake 5 minutes longer or until cheese is melted. Let stand 10 minutes before serving. *Makes 6 servings*

Betty Jo's Sausage and Cheese Grits

WESSON® No-Stick Cooking Spray
1 pound mild or hot cooked sausage, crumbled and drained
1½ cups grits
2½ cups shredded Cheddar cheese
3 tablespoons WESSON® Vegetable Oil
1½ cups milk
3 eggs, slightly beaten

Preheat oven to 350°F. Lightly spray 13×9×2-inch baking dish with Wesson Cooking Spray. Evenly spread crumbled sausage on bottom of dish; set aside. Bring 4½ cups water to a boil in a large saucepan. Stir in grits and lower heat. Cook 5 minutes until thickened, stirring occasionally. Add cheese and Wesson Oil; stir until cheese has melted. Stir in milk and eggs; blend well. Evenly spoon mixture over sausage; bake, uncovered, 1 hour or until grits have set. *Makes 6 to 8 servings*

Cheddar cheese is easier to shred if it's cold.

Cheesy Country SPAM™ Puff

Lightened Up

Mini Vegetable Quiches

2 cups assorted cut-up
    vegetables
2 tablespoons chopped green
    onions
2 tablespoons FLEISCHMANN'S®
    Original Spread (70% Corn
    Oil)

4 (8-inch) flour tortillas, each
    cut into 8 triangles
1 cup EGG BEATERS® Healthy
    Real Egg Substitute
1 cup fat-free (skim) milk
½ teaspoon dried basil leaves

In medium nonstick skillet, over medium-high heat, sauté vegetables and
green onions in spread until tender. Arrange 4 tortilla pieces in each of 8 (6-
ounce) greased custard cups or ramekins, placing points of tortilla pieces at
center of bottom of cup and pressing lightly to form shape of cup. Divide
vegetable mixture evenly among cups. In small bowl, combine Egg Beaters®,
milk and basil. Pour evenly over vegetable mixture. Place cups on baking
sheet. Bake at 375°F for 20 to 25 minutes or until puffed and knife inserted
into centers comes out clean. Let stand 5 minutes before serving.

Makes 8 servings

Nutrients per Serving: Calories 122, Total Fat 4 g, Cholesterol 1 mg, Sodium 198 mg

Oven Breakfast Hash

2 pounds baking potatoes, unpeeled
    (5 or 6 medium)
1 pound BOB EVANS® Original
    Recipe Roll Sausage
1 (12-ounce can) evaporated milk
⅓ cup chopped green onions
1 tablespoon Worcestershire sauce
½ teaspoon salt
¼ teaspoon black pepper
¼ cup dried bread crumbs
1 tablespoon melted butter or
    margarine
½ teaspoon paprika

Cook potatoes in boiling water until
fork-tender. Drain and coarsely chop or
mash. Preheat oven to 350°F. Crumble
and cook sausage in medium skillet
until browned. Drain and transfer to
large bowl. Stir in potatoes, milk, green
onions, Worcestershire sauce, salt and
pepper. Pour into greased 2½- or
3-quart casserole dish. Sprinkle with
bread crumbs; drizzle with melted
butter. Sprinkle with paprika. Bake,
uncovered, 30 to 35 minutes.

Makes 6 to 8 servings

Mini Vegetable Quiches

Acknowledgments

The publisher would like to thank the companies and organizations listed below for the use of their recipes and photographs in this publication.

Alpine Lace Brands, Inc.

Birds Eye®

Bob Evans®

Butterball® Turkey Company

COLLEGE INN® Broth

Colorado Potato Administrative Committee

Delmarva Poultry Industry, Inc.

Del Monte Corporation

EGG BEATERS® Healthy Real Egg Substitute

Equal® sweetener

Filippo Berio Olive Oil

FLEISCHMANN'S® Original Spread

Florida Department of Agriculture and Consumer Services, Bureau of Seafood and Aquaculture

Golden Grain®

GREY POUPON® Mustard

Guiltless Gourmet®

Healthy Choice®

Hillshire Farm®

Hormel Foods Corporation

Hunt-Wesson, Inc.

The J.M. Smucker Company

Kikkoman International Inc.

Kraft Foods, Inc.

Lawry's® Foods, Inc.

Minnesota Cultivated Wild Rice Council

MOTT'S® Inc., a division of Cadbury Beverages Inc.

National Honey Board

National Pork Producers Council

Nestlé USA, Inc.

Norseland, Inc.

North Dakota Beef Commission

Reckitt & Colman Inc.

StarKist® Seafood Company

INDEX

Metric Conversion Chart

VOLUME MEASUREMENTS (dry)

$\frac{1}{8}$ teaspoon = 0.5 mL
$\frac{1}{4}$ teaspoon = 1 mL
$\frac{1}{2}$ teaspoon = 2 mL
$\frac{3}{4}$ teaspoon = 4 mL
1 teaspoon = 5 mL
1 tablespoon = 15 mL
2 tablespoons = 30 mL
$\frac{1}{4}$ cup = 60 mL
$\frac{1}{3}$ cup = 75 mL
$\frac{1}{2}$ cup = 125 mL
$\frac{2}{3}$ cup = 150 mL
$\frac{3}{4}$ cup = 175 mL
1 cup = 250 mL
2 cups = 1 pint = 500 mL
3 cups = 750 mL
4 cups = 1 quart = 1 L

VOLUME MEASUREMENTS (fluid)

1 fluid ounce (2 tablespoons) = 30 mL
4 fluid ounces ($\frac{1}{2}$ cup) = 125 mL
8 fluid ounces (1 cup) = 250 mL
12 fluid ounces (1$\frac{1}{2}$ cups) = 375 mL
16 fluid ounces (2 cups) = 500 mL

WEIGHTS (mass)

$\frac{1}{2}$ ounce = 15 g
1 ounce = 30 g
3 ounces = 90 g
4 ounces = 120 g
8 ounces = 225 g
10 ounces = 285 g
12 ounces = 360 g
16 ounces = 1 pound = 450 g

DIMENSIONS

$\frac{1}{16}$ inch = 2 mm
$\frac{1}{8}$ inch = 3 mm
$\frac{1}{4}$ inch = 6 mm
$\frac{1}{2}$ inch = 1.5 cm
$\frac{3}{4}$ inch = 2 cm
1 inch = 2.5 cm

OVEN TEMPERATURES

250°F = 120°C
275°F = 140°C
300°F = 150°C
325°F = 160°C
350°F = 180°C
375°F = 190°C
400°F = 200°C
425°F = 220°C
450°F = 230°C

BAKING PAN SIZES

Utensil	Size in Inches/Quarts	Metric Volume	Size in Centimeters
Baking or Cake Pan (square or rectangular)	8×8×2	2 L	20×20×5
	9×9×2	2.5 L	23×23×5
	12×8×2	3 L	30×20×5
	13×9×2	3.5 L	33×23×5
Loaf Pan	8×4×3	1.5 L	20×10×7
	9×5×3	2 L	23×13×7
Round Layer Cake Pan	8×1½	1.2 L	20×4
	9×1½	1.5 L	23×4
Pie Plate	8×1¼	750 mL	20×3
	9×1¼	1 L	23×3
Baking Dish or Casserole	1 quart	1 L	—
	1½ quart	1.5 L	—
	2 quart	2 L	—